Thirty-Seven
A book of poems

by Jason Tomlinson

Hendersonville, Tennessee

Thirty-seven: a book of poems
by Jason Tomlinson
©2016 Jason Tomlinson

All rights reserved. Printed in the United States of America. No part of this publication may be reproduced without the permission of the copyright holder.

ISBN: 978-1-365-19903-5

Jason Tomlinson
www.bringbackthepoetry.com

For Landon, Hannah and Nathan

Introduction

In the fall of 1993 I lived in Burton, Michigan where I was a 15 year old sophomore at Valley Christian Academy. Around that time I had joined the staff of Word Up, a section of the Flint Journal that appeared every Sunday. At Word Up students were encouraged to submit all sorts of articles and write-ups including poetry. The creative atmosphere among the Word Up writers was just the sort that was ideal for me to write my first poem. So, one day in biology, I cranked out my first, Outcast's Cry. It was instant satisfaction and I've never looked back.

In the fall of 1996 I was a freshman at Lipscomb University in Nashville, Tennessee. I discovered The Owl's Nest, a coffee shop on 22nd. They had a monthly poetry open mic and I went to the first one I could. Once again, the satisfaction I felt rhyming in front of people was complete. I went as often as I could and enjoyed the encouragement and camaraderie of the other poets there who amazed me on a regular basis.

In the fall of 2001 I was a Junior at Harding University in Searcy, Arkansas. Leah and I had been married a little more than a year and life was really, really good. We had purchased our first desktop computer and soon after I picked a loop based music program called Acid Music by Sonic Foundry. I had the idea of making a spoken word album with experimental background music. In late 2001, I produced my first album, *I'm Doing Something Different Tonight.* Making the album was a delight and with its creation I began to pursue regular gigs at schools, churches, camps, coffee shops and bars. During this time I discovered the Little Rock Poetry Slam which was one of the most important tools that shaped me as a young aspiring spoken word artist. The atmosphere was both hostile and nurturing and I will never forget some of the words I heard and people I met while there.

In the fall of 2010 I had ultimately given up on the idea of being a career spoken word artist. Many things contributed to this, some good some bad but I was mistaken. Though I may never make much money writing and performing I will never be done and that's a comforting and empowering thought. In August of 2010 I competed in Community's Got Talent at the Community Church of Hendersonville. I used my old favorite stand-by, Alliterate Adoration, and in the middle of being on stage something came alive inside me that had not been stirred for years.

On December 2, 2014 I turned 37 and on that day I made a sporadic decision that proved to be valuable. I resolved to write and post a poem everyday and I nearly did just that. It woke up my creativity to a degree I'd never known. It lead me to being more observant, grateful and aware. Since creativity isn't content to be to be an only child my poetry found other avenues to occupy including live shows, youtube videos, open mics, and even my own podcast. As a result, you now have the poems I wrote on my 37th trip around the sun in your hands. I strongly encourage you to pull any of them up on my website as there are no small amount of pictures for thematic support and audio for the interviews I conducted with all of the tributes.

Now, as a husband, father and middle school teacher I am tempted to believe that I don't have time for poetry but these three roles that God has given me serve to spur on my creativity as strong as it has ever been. I reckon I'll keep on writing, rhyming, recording and performing. Enjoy

Power

Our imagination is insufficient to possibly comprehend
our potential to attack and our potential to defend
our influence is immeasurable due to our branding
our soul's mark simply means nothing is too demanding
for what we have is a light that cannot fade
untouchable it was in us the moment we were made
the strength that endures through every season and year
we call it power on display right here

Pass it On

In so many ways I've received satisfaction
from so many who gave me life long traction
to trek through the landscape of all these years
amid laughter heartache pain and tears
to a place where I could turn and do the same for others
empowered to serve in the same way for my young brothers
and the gratitude that wells up even stronger as of late
leads me to persevere and perpetuate
this good thing so that it will never be gone
this good thing I've been given
here
pass it on

The Grip

When it comes to reality I don't exactly have the best grip
ne'er a day goes by that I don't find some way to trip
the discouragement can be immense
      overwhelming soul to bone
so thankful I don't have to imagine doing a bit of it alone
surrounded by the four of you
      we bear one another's wrongs
we fight one another's battles and listen to our songs
the happy verses and sad dirges
      are ours to appreciate exclusively
battles won chains undone so glad you men are there for me

Snapshot

I don't remember being fed by my mom and dad when I was just a little dude
but I can't forget the beauty and wonder of seeing my dad give my son his food
it's like a snapshot of the care that I've received every single day
I remember and I am blessed in such memories I'll stay
God's love precedes my ability to recall
nurtured loved and surrounded He's provided through it all

Beautiful Declaration

The order of words could be interpreted either way
so punctuation is imperative for precision in what I say
without it the meaning would be lost in ambiguity
but because of it anyone who reads
      can clearly understand me
that's pretty much how life is here
these words and this sentence are these months and this year
but it is all lost unless you're a part of it
while you are not all you certainly are the heart of it
the punctuation the frame by which
      everything is understood
the perception of what is bad
      the discernment for what is good
thank you for the conclusions questions
      lists and exclamations
thank you for turning every day into a beautiful declaration

The Richest Life

The paradoxes of seeking to fill one's self are deceptive indeed
for the void created by engaging in greed
can only be compared to gulping water at sea
and the effort for hydration becomes impossibility
but conversely it is interesting that satisfaction takes place
in not seeking to seize stuff and stuff one's face
but in liberally strewing resources everywhere
just sharing the good with little to no care
for what is retained for the one giving
and in this way there is made a living
a living far richer than hoarding could ever be
the richest life made possible by generosity

Not For Sale

It's not for sale
It's impossible to steal
There's nothing I'd trade it for
And circumstances don't dictate it

Wallowing in the Riches

I cannot begin to sum up how wealthy she makes me feel
I'm a king perhaps a thief life with her is a steal
and I don't care what happens I'm not giving her back
She's mine and I'm hers and we're on the same track
with a few bumps it's true but we never derail
more than anything I'd say that she and I sail
over waves of stress fear and regret
we're back home now and you can bet
that we'll stay right here surrounded by charms
wallowing in the riches of each other's arms

Hide Myself

No theme has greater frequency than this one I so often return
of all the opportunities seized and lost
      there's one thing I've managed to learn
and that is simply to trust that You are enough
In the ebb and flow the smooth and the rough
the disappointments and trespasses the friends gone away
the moment I just don't know what to say
I return to this theme when nothing but trouble is in view
I return to these words and hide myself in You

Show Us

You are right You have always been right
Maker of Heaven and Earth sky seas and light
immeasurable in your goodness wisdom and strength
no limits to Your depth no end to Your length
the Ancient of Days I Am Who I Am and always will be
Inventor of all that we hear, touch and see
all these things are so all bear witness true
but this time of year I'm inclined to think so much more of You
cause from the dawn of time You have been leading
giving us all exactly just what we were needing
it's been this way from times older than old
we needed to know and it was You who told
us just how to live and just what to do
from Abraham to Malachi we were able to hear from You
but better than telling us from town to town
You picked the time and the place and You came down
You came down in order to know us
born in humility just to show us
everything that had been written from day one
is the Word made flesh   Messiah   Son

Emerging in Emergency

We need Him
and that's a good thing
we long for His Presence
we were made to
He shows up unexpectedly
emerging in emergency
urgently in urgency
to provide and meet needs
we could never articulate
it's beautiful
He is beautiful
and though He was on no one's list
He is the gift we all want and need
freely given new traditions are established
and life can be understood in better ways
may we all understand His better way

Family Grace

Irreplaceable to the greatest degree
impossible to describe what they mean to me
snuggles kisses and hugs lavished abundantly
all the above just for my family

Their attention and affection is my favorite song
365 all year long
even on days when everything goes wrong
this act ain't never gonna get the gong

Cause what would I take to put in their place
no sight compares to seeing their face
no touch compares to their embrace
Indeed they manifest the very Presence of Grace

Star Light

I see all these points of light shining in the night sky of my day
each one an important memory of someone along the way
I try to connect the stars into a mental constellation
but it is a futile attempt as there is no such organization
these random blessings are no less significant though
over the years I've noticed and I have come to know
that without these stars these points of light
I am lost in endless night
but with them everything is crystal clear
these stars are the memories that have brought me here

Restore the Broken

There's not a one of us that Life hasn't overspent
its aches and pains never relent
to the point where all is overdrawn
and it seems all goodness all hope is gone
indeed our own identification is rooted in what we've lost
unable to cope with these circumstances unable to cover the
        cost
left dry with less than nothing alone in the cold
it's so familiar it is so old
it needs to be better it needs to be more
it wants to stand up and walk even though weak and sore
a whisper uttered in the stillness stirs something unknown
or perhaps just forgotten but all the same currently unsown
what is this? who is this? who treads the roads mile marked
        with grief?
who makes the difference for those foreign to relief?
who restores the broken with renewed confidence?
who defies logic and refutes evidence?
the clouded perspective held by me and you
who is this that makes everything new?

The Pay Off

Strength follows weakness when revealed honestly
It is not fun at first
It is more-or-less a pain
but the pay off is something much more still
and can only be partaken of by those who have revealed
Someone texted to check up on me today
and I cannot tell you how much it was worth
the idea that me acknowledging my weaknesses out loud
is a good one therefore I raise the stakes
I endeavor to quit the old and embrace what's right
not alone not ever alone
I am surrounded by forces much bigger than I

Never Return Again

Some adventures change us in ways that cannot be undone
accomplishment leads us beyond the setting sun
to lands far away and sights unexpected
but we succeeded and good was directed
toward those that needed assistance
we finished the work with tenacious persistence
but when we came home we were caught unaware
that in such comfort it was weird to be there
not that anyone or anything was mean in any way
nor did anyone have an unkind word to say
but we were different from the moment we came
for adventures never leave its participants the same
it changes them forever all women and men
we go home in body only for our hearts can never return again

Staying Right Here

This is my story
at least it is the beginning
I'm just a few chapters into it
but I already feel like I'm winning
not because I'm good or smart I'm certainly not the best
but when I think about it I can't help feeling extraordinarily blessed
my Father has poured out His Spirit through His Son
Salvation is mine because of Him not at all what I've done
and in addition to it all this I journey with my crew
my team allow me to introduce my few

Given the option of being with anyone in the whole universe
you can probably guess my answer based on this verse
cause the chorus is the same as verses one two and three
there are none better there are no substitutes for me
but just the real thing that she is appears to be and does
these and so many more are the reasons because
our destinies have been woven together by the Master Weaver
and in dark days and black nights I will never leave her
but by her side in my arms in the sunshine and rain
here. always. we remain
persevering enduring stitched up by love's knitting
by a thread Divine we are made one by One greater
it makes a difference now it'll make a difference later
to the end of our days when its just me and her
and in that late hour one thing will occur
at least one thing I can say this for sure
not because either one of us is pure
nor because we have such a great amount of care
but we will make it because He will be there

But seriously that is a long ways away
we have no shortage of things going on today
these three have blown up our lives every year
specifically for example is this one right here

I LOVE THIS GUY! Seriously! He's like no other
growing up so fast he's getting to be like a brother
hanging out with him is never a bore
or a chore he's so cool I'll take time with him galore
from his beginning out west in the Golden State
my big boy Landon! that dude? SO GREAT!

Speaking of great Landon has a sister
and you would be amiss if you happened to miss her
so allow me to introduce this little lass
the princess of pizzazz little miss sass
she is my baby girl positively perfect in every way
possessing a magical spirit that carries every day
shining bright a delight for whom everyone cares
though still her own person never putting on heirs
but confident with every step respected in every place
my Hannah Elizabeth representative of Grace

And now to this boy not at all to be outdone
my little fella cutest of all is my baby boy son
to a degree I did not realize existed
but now I bear witness as I've seen it persisted
every day and I see him he's the world to me
he's not quite two and already I can see
the impact that he's had on everyone he comes across
smiles invade every encounter he's a little boss
and he commands happiness to suddenly appear
every day is blessed I thank God he's here

Every day is blessed because of all five
each one of us is blessed just to be alive
and be next to involved in with one another
husband wife sister brother
united and wrapped up given by He
who gave us to each other me for you you for me

unstoppable together charging down opposition
refusing to entertain any other proposition
committed with reservations for every single year
my God my family I'm staying right here

Needs to Be Said

I don't know if I can say this the way it needs to be said
but I'm inclined to speak what's in my heart and head
the truth of the matter is these thoughts are pretty old
so it's high time I told you cause to me you're solid gold

I admire you in the truest sense of the word
your drive focus and determination remain undeterred
by setbacks that would bury a weaker heart
but your steel is evident in every part
and that's why you're worthy of congratulation
that's why you have my undying admiration

I honor you for how far you've come
I know where you stand and I know where you're from
and the distance in between is the east to the west
now this side of hard work you've earned some rest
I would consider myself successful if I ended up just like you
I offer up honor your example is a great view

I'm proud of you I brag about you a lot
your ethic and perseverance are worth being caught
by any and everyone wanting to succeed
your commitment to discipline is commitment indeed
so I have so much hope for your generation
your true spirit defying expectation
let's me know you know what to do
for these and so many reasons are why I'm so proud of you

I love you there is no other more important to me
you alone are the one with whom I always want to be
for reasons I can understand and for some I cannot
my love for you is greater than anything I've thought
there's a mystery to it I wouldn't have it any other way
I love you so much you're my night you're my day

Reconciled

When things go wrong sometimes people say
that irreconcilable differences left no way
for things to have gone the way they should
so we shut it down cause it's just no good
better to call dead things dead there's no need to trip
call it off there is no longer any relationship

All of this is based in painful familiarity
it's break my heart reality with zero hilarity
two offended parties going separate ways
hoping the exit yields better future days
satisfied in one way glad to be out
but unsatisfied in another ever entertaining doubt
what if we hadn't chosen relationship's elimination?
what if somehow there could've been reconciliation?

That's what we wonder is it not?
don't we imagine these battles fought
yielding themselves to something more fulfilling
and not just a scenario with everyone so unwilling
I suppose a requirement over right and wrong
would be more about which one is strong
and that would be strong in terms of righteousness
thus creating a great need for forgiveness
so hard to give especially when right
but there's nothing else that will bring the light
of healing when one has issued offense
and no longer has any defense
but is simply at the mercy of the one offended
the only one who can prevent its being ended

I know of no greater offense than that of the Divine
Who extended forgiveness when I crossed the line
the relationship was salvaged it did not go away
though my actions lacked merit He chose to let me stay
He said that I am His child
that's why this season means so much
God and sinners reconciled

Gifts

Sometimes I think these eyes are mine
but such thoughts leave me far from fine
for seeking to fill my eyes is no way to live
they are gifts so their purpose is to give

Sometimes I think this tongue is for my speech
when I do I am the witness of satisfaction's breach
this tongue for my words is no way to live
speech is for Your words only Your words give

Sometimes I think these hands are for taking
such thoughts betray I'm prone to peace forsaking
for hands that take are no way to live
these hands' sole purpose is naught but to give

Sometimes I think these steps belong to me
such notions steal me from where I want to be
determining my steps is no way to live
don't take these steps these steps I give

In Defense of Defense

Conflict is inevitable regardless the matter
like the baseball coming straight at the batter
there's not necessarily someone to blame
just like life it's part of the game
so rest assured it's unavoidable for sure
though for a season one may endure
without a fight from a friend or foe
but before long that's how it'll go
don't worry though I have good news
there is one measure we all can use
lest we fret and become too tense
there is much to be said in defense of defense
it is inevitable that we'll all meet our end
and choose whether to attack or defend
I say defend again and again
in the world of boys and the world of men
a good defense trumps a good offense every day
the reasons are many but let me say
that one important reason why defense is best
Is that defense moves from a place of rest
while offense was moving bound over bound
defense was secure standing its ground
ready for peace to come undone
and when the smoke cleared defense won

Cry for Peace

In every corner of every nation
every story speaks desperation
with no limits and no potential to cease
the whole Earth cries out
the whole Earth wants peace
sometimes these cries are heard in some pretty scary ways
these cries are uttered after many dark nights and days
and peace starved people have limited reaction
but only peace will give us satisfaction
only peace can get us through
and only peace means only You

Gifts are for Sharing

These gifts are an absolute pleasure
to be enjoyed fully they are a treasure
to be used by as many as possibly can
not just a few but quite a wide span
of all kinds of people in all kinds of places
resulting in tears of joy and bright faces
reflecting the Light through actions declaring
these gifts are only ours for sharing

Light Me Up

This year's Christmas tree was not exactly the best
the shape was very different it wasn't like the rest
of the living trees that we have had so many years before
no the unfortunate shape of this year's tree left us wanting something more
here's the thing though – it wasn't a total waste
I found improved perspective that reformed my taste
for the tree actually took on a different form
and there was this one thing that improved its norm
we were happy in the living room many nights
for the tree looked great dressed up in lights
the lights lassoed around the Christmas tree
made it shine beautifully
not unlike some of us
who argue complain fight and fuss
but turn for the better clothed in Light
so seeing them is actually a real delight
Lord light me up like a unsightly tree
so I can bless all who come by me
let my stature be Light's frame for all year
so the world will know You are here

Home Right Here

It scared me to death!
so loud and sudden it stole my breath
I had to step away for the sake of sanity
shock set in it got the best of me
I only wanted to go home and just be done
none of this had turned out none of it was fun
I turned to the only source of comfort from such harms
tears dropping arms wrapping I fled to father's arms
no we weren't home yet but he was home right here
I could hold on to him even while in fear
I knew he was enough 'til it was time to leave
his presence was my peace to receive
he absorbed my fear the shock ceased to grow
and my heart found rest when he said to me "come on, it's time to go"

Defiant Survival

She was planted in a place contrary to flourishing
significant obstacles challenged her nourishing
it wasn't her fault life began in such a place
but her perspective would be her race
and whether or not she would finish would be her choice
since her world wasn't tuned to hear her voice
the odds were against her staying alive
so she defied them to survive
because of this she didn't quite fit in
and her refusal to cooperate rendered a win
she defied expectations and brilliantly got it done
leaving it all behind she arrived in the sun

Bounty

The God of five loaves and two fish is still here
He is the same this year and last year
we do a little and He does beyond measure
we do spare change He does crazy treasure

There was a Saturday morning I can use as an example
His performance as usual was perfectly ample
to give you an idea of what I'm saying
so you too can pass on these words conveying
the boxes were coming my direction
and we were making this awesome collection
of food to give away for those in need
so impressive were those in the lead
and they admitted being impressed too
for our hours to complete the job were a few
until about 400 were stacked against the wall
what a sight! we had a ball!
now here's the kicker the big surprise
the folks in charge directed our eyes
to stuff for us! is this for real?!
oh my word! what a deal!
I walked over to see what was good for taking
and then I saw it - my hands started shaking
I couldn't believe that it wasn't a gag
five pounds of Starbucks beans in a bag!
now days later it's a daily reminder
that God's kindness is ever kinder
these beans from the food bank in Sumner County
testify to the riches of God's great bounty

Escape Engage

The severity of the paradox comes down to the minute
it's so subtle you may not know you're in it
cause intentions were made but not followed through
and distractions have made a fool of you
and me too it's a common condition
these devices mix up subtraction and addition
the story is confusing page to page
cause sometimes we escape and sometimes we engage
we're either pursuing or avoiding some situation
plugging in or disconnecting some social relation
God co-workers family and friends
cutting em off or making amends
I must be careful to specifically mention
that both have value when its your intention
to escape or engage is actually okay
these gadgets serve their purpose night and day
discretion and discernment will lead healthy action
so your tech doesn't cost you points of attraction
or rest these devices can be great for me and you
provided we're doing what we intended to do

Indestructible

I've got friends family foes and fans
in numerous cities and multiple lands
and for every last individual I offer up thanks
my life is richer than savings in a thousand banks
your contributions and investments into my soul
propel me on to my daily goal
of doing being and achieving more
looking forward to what's in store
but right now let me dial it down a bit
and narrow the focus to my greatest hit
to the most important person in my life
by now you gotta know I'm talking 'bout my wife!
cause honestly I love my friends I really do
but she's the one that gets me through
my buddies and my bros can help me start
but my woman is my beating heart
when her hug and kiss send me out the door
I'm ready to take on the whole world in war
cause her support respect and admiration
are worthy of this year end celebration
she believes in me and that gets me going
like I'm bullet proof on the mic while I'm flowing
and rhyming she says "baby, you can"
I'm ten feet fall cause I'm her man
she's my number one fan and because of this
I feel like there's nothing I can miss
I'm impossible to drown in any tide
I'm indestructible cause she is by my side

Now

"This will be the year I. . ." forget about it
success in nebulous plans? I doubt it
my annual resolutions reveal procrastination's heart
in attempts to quit or to start
claiming 12 months at a time is a tall order
Really! Success demands something much shorter
annual monthly weekly and daily are really just too much
the limits of our little hands are understood
touch by touch
let's make these changes – here's how
break it down to the moment let's do it right now
our years months weeks and days are not guaranteed
I can't say what'll happen can't say where they'll lead
but right now is magic with all the right stuff
now is perfect now is enough

Fan

It's great to watch a fan excited
cheer on her team they're winning she's delighted
she's mighty fine company to be around
her team just made another touch-down
I'm a winner watching her cheer
watching her watch them I'm so glad to be here
her team is winning her faith rewarded
broadcasting happy with gladness recorded
Friday night victory is the plan
she's watching I'm smiling sure do love my fan

Strike Me Down
(In Memory of Obi-Wan Kenobi)

In a moment I felt a great disturbance in the Force
millions were silenced in one swift course
the strength of such evil was foreign to me
I didn't know of such atrocities such severity
the Dark Side was much darker than I thought
an end must be made before further harm is wrought
I feel the Force leading me to a place of surrender
a plan forms in my mind and I will be the sender
of freedom for those who will finish the fight
no battle station will subdue the Light
I shut down the pull so my friends can go
and I am confronted by a powerful foe
A Master of Evil stands in my way
intent on making this my last day
he wants to kill me and I will permit it
because he really doesn't get it
he can't imagine how powerful I will be
when he strikes me down but already I can see
just What the Force wants to accomplish here
in victory I surrender and swiftly disappear

Face the Sun

Our limits frequently inhibit our perception
as our senses lead us to subtle deception
for we suppose at the close of every day
that the sun sets as it goes away
but truthfully the sun never sets nor does it rise
despite what we see with our own two eyes
something much more wondrous is taking place
the sun doesn't move but the Earth will face
the source of heat and light for our blue sphere
the marker of time in our atmosphere
and there is beauty in why we face the other way
it's all about sharing our night is the day
of the other side of the world I don't mind at all
sharing these resources with everyone on this ball
it reminds me that every time I face the sun
I am by no means the only one
who can behold it's beauty while I watch it in the air
and I wonder just now what else can I share?

Lesser Became Greater (Bilbo's Poem)

An unexpected party started the greatest adventure he ever took
any other day he'd be sitting by the fire reading a book
but one wiser than he chose him for the task
even though he certainly did not ask
for the two sides of his personality didn't have equal share
and the dominant one would never dare
do what the lesser one longed to do
but the lesser became greater and that's how he got through
the first thing he faced concerned a peculiar whim
of hungry trolls leaving roast mutton and choosing instead to feast on him
and his friends but luck wisdom sunshine and wit
overturned the trolls' attempts they didn't get a bit
so the fifteen were soon on their way
to a short rest for many a night and many a day
the Last Homely House where they stayed as guest
Lord Elrond gave them respite from their quest
supplied with food drink story and song
and complete protection from all things wrong
they stayed there in Rivendell for many days and nights
until the day came for them to leave those happy lights
and go out over hill and under hill as well
horrible things lived down in where they fell
but they were rescued once again by a wizard's spark
and a magic ring was won by a match of riddles in the dark
but if I told you they were doing well I would be a liar
as they were out of the frying-pan into the fire
of goblins and wargs united set on evil to bring
but the wizard organized transportation on the back of eagle's wing
to lead them to queer lodgings what an interesting place!
their skin-changing host had more than one face

the bear-man was frightening but ultimately good
and he prepared them for their trek through Mirkwood
like flies and spiders they were the prey
and it is true they all would've died that day
had it not been for him and his ring
such cleverness displayed with his courage and sting
but the victory was brief as they would be caught
by suspicious elves who didn't trust them a lot
or at all really but drunken elves were conned
by the invisible thief with barrels out of bond
on to a warm welcome by nearly all around
the hospitality was great right there in Lake Town
they re-fueled there it was so great to see
soon they were on the doorstep of their mighty enemy
he seemed impenetrable invincible he had wrought such desolation
but a little bird was listening and delivered inside information
the enemy was unaware his weakness had been been made known
so he took off for war and death leaving the company alone
they were confused for a while and soon began to roam
for they couldn't understand why the dragon was not at home
but fire and water collided when the archer heard what was said
one arrow black and true – the great dragon was dead
all would've been won the journey done that day
but complications arose and lead to another way
the gathering of the clouds signaled battle's call
even though a thief in the night was put out with it all
such stubbornness was inexcusable in his well earned opinion
he was tired beyond description and sick of being a minion
but foes became allies as the goblins did their worst

for at the battle of five armies through violence the clouds burst
tears were shed amends were made and ultimately good won
many things happened on the mountain that could not be undone
the impact would be felt for the rest of his days
the consequences would impact all of his ways
at last the day came for the return journey back
his experiences and treasure filled much more than his pack
but his mind was filled for his story would be written page after page
quill ink and paper would be passed
    for this would not be the last stage

Dream

He is mine come true I can't thank God too much
his sounds how he looks how he moves his touch
such feelings well up both bright and deep
as I watch this little wonder fast asleep
I imagine what visions pass through his mind
things both amazing and kind
sweet words spoken and heartfelt affection
love courage and faith all in his direction
he dreams for himself and I dream for him too
my dream is my prayer for his future view
I see his path paved with indescribable peace
his joy and faithfulness will never cease
for they will be filled from an infinite supply
his Heavenly Father will be with him by and by
so I know my dream for him is not in vain
my dream will shield him in the wind and the rain
we dream these dreams we anticipate the view
of glory in the morning when these dreams come true

Heart Filled

Unexpected solitude is rarely fun
to have plans and then be the only one
who shows up at the time and place
the whole thing gives me a downcast face
and I sit alone still as can be
and frequently my thoughts turn to me
but this time feels different from the start
cause I remember I'm not the only one in my heart
I have plenty of company inside
the depth and breadth is deep and wide
the experiences and individuals that are there everyday
drive the loneliness in my solitude far far away
so the purpose of my solitude is spent in reflection
and self-pity is acknowledged as vain deception
for the restlessness in my heart is stilled
when in silence I realize how my heart is filled

Days that Count

I used to spend my days in temptation's crosshairs
avoiding mistakes consumed my cares
counting the days I didn't get shot
which most of the time weren't really a lot
not doing that thing I considered so wrong
monopolized every verse of my song
I've got a different song now it's new and improved
failing methods have now been moved
to the margins while I've turned loose and started running
with a pursuit for excellence you could say I'm gunning
'cause targets are falling before my eyes
I now count the days I seize the prize
I count the days I am winning
these days of righteousness and not not sinning
as I count I do much more than simply survive
these days that I count are the days I'm alive

Side by Side (A Tribute to Robin)

My first son my protégé successor and ward
the source in which my hope is stored
turning flips while smiling in the face of fear
I knew you as a boy now I know you as a peer
a proud hero who holds a valiant fight
side by side we shine in the dark night

The most unlikely candidate for the post
with qualities not quite obvious to most
I welcomed you to a better day
for years it was great until you went away
my world in an instant blown apart
your departure destroyed my heart
but your return marked a new page
as evil now flees before your rage

The smartest one yet the brightest kid
you knew what I needed more than I did
you saw the vacancy and witnessed the need
and critically you delivered indeed
I've saved many but you saved me
you were exactly what I needed you to be
now shaded red your own course to direct
just know forever you have a my respect

Mysterious and violent unmistakably blazing
indeed my son though not of my raising
but come from a world far far away
geographically emotionally pretty much in every way
but your style and your moves prove we are kin
you stand out among the other young men
for a season you were gone and a part of me died
now you're back never leave always fight by my side

Show Up

The road to 10,000 isn't paved
it's not even cleared it must be braved
by the fearless few who dare engage
the uncharted land with no guided page
tenacious consistency defying feeling
the load would send the weaker reeling
but the strong remain because of this
this one thing so many others miss
when others flounder when they need to grow up
perseverance propels and they just show up
it's their practice it's their habit it's their nature consistent
it's their will it's their pattern it's course so persistent
no plateaus just inclines and strides to do better
they show up cause they are the definition of go getter
they practice practice practice everywhere they're at
I remind myself of these role models cause I wanna be like that

The Sad Poem

Sometimes I need a sad poem
a story of love lost
a collection of hopelessness
a cry for the dead
a grievance for what is gone
I don't want to hear that it's going to get better
I don't want any silver linings
and I don't want to find the positive angle
I just want to feel this sadness

The Key Person

We were tossing out attempts to no avail
the doldrums threatened our potential to sail
but fresh wind was soon felt in the frustrating air
and the four of us took off right there
it was as if the whole thing had been planned
by Someone higher this couldn'ta been manned
we all smiled at the touch of grace
so nice to have a key person in place

Christmas Ghosts

The tree is down the stockings are packed and the company
    is gone
Three weeks past Christmas and yet the holiday goes on
the house is quiet but I am not alone
for unseen guests haunt my house and they are all well
    known
they come every year to remind me where I'm from
they are my Christmas ghosts and I'm so glad they've come
for their visits serve not to frighten
but rather to console and enlighten
the physical reminders i display this time of year
are pointers to their presence - they are here
and I hear them softly whisper to me
practice kindness practice gratitude practice generosity
I close my eyes and listen while shedding a tear
so glad to have heard them so glad that they are here

We Could Be Friends

We're here together every day
and it's highly likely this is where we'll stay
so while we're here we could make the most of it
and figure out a few ways of how we could boast of it
because we're gonna be logging a lot of hours here
so let's lose frowns and add smiles every year
let's secure sweetness for all of our ends
my idea? we could be friends
we could be more than workers in this place
more than employees taking up office space
more than managers, nurses, doctors and technicians
pastors plumbers or electricians
we could choose a more noble association
than the fact that we have the same vocation
more than the same way our work day spends
wanna have lunch? 'cause we could be friends

Lay Down My Word

All these words go only so far
their limits are quick to appear
the range within their motion is par
they can only do so much here
I pick these words every day
in order to express feeling
I carefully craft them so what I say
will bring understanding and healing
my intentions are true
they are love and attraction
but to really get through
it's gonna take action
saying it is nothing compared to it showing
words can't get that much stirred
I for one want everyone knowing
so gladly I lay down my word

The Balloon Poem

Balloons are
secret agents
of happiness
sent by the good guys
to save your day
use them often

Body Part

All the parts of my body got the perfect part
cast as the good guys
it was perfect from the start
from head to toe I was created for good things
excellence and performance
all the best fit for kings
but sometimes I would forget
the role for which I was cast
and reminders would be sent so I could last
and make it to the end of the story
giving my Director the full measure of glory
my body part was never meant to malign
nor was it meant to sit around
and simply be benign
the part every part got from skin to nerve
was hero and protector I got the part to serve

Implications and Consequences

The neglect to consider implications in the past
has lead to these consequences here at last
so my current considerations have been refined
to include such matters in my mind
since tomorrow is built on today
giving heed to implications is a much better way
there's no need for consequences to be so misunderstood
on the contrary they could be good
all courses could end in celebrations
provided I consider my action's implications

Little Ones

These little ones are in good hands
their present is protected as well as future plans
by the Shepherd who watches their every motion
their needs occupy His loving devotion
so they don't worry about a thing
'cause they know just what the Shepherd can bring
and it defies all thought and imagination
they trust in Him Who erases all frustration
good times are here and more are on the way
I'm watching what they're doing and hearing what they say
and what they say is gold I don't wanna miss a thing
every day is a wonder every day is something to bring
an offering of happiness the laughter is consistent
heartaches only temporary hugs are more persistent
my eyes are wide open to all of this right here
I know how fast it goes every single year
I blink and its way too fast
so in joy I meditate to make it all last
and even though it's temporary
which in some ways can be scary
I find one thing that gets me through
the Shepherd guides them beyond my view
such awareness leads me to smile
casting my worry in big pile
of irrelevant things I'll never use
with such advantages I'll never lose
infinity to zero my team's record is perfection
firm foundation guaranteed there is no better direction
the hope for these little ones is great
    just look Who's doing the sending
the Shepherd's kindness and wisdom is evident
    indeed His Love is unending

Call Him Dad

Many call him brother since he brings the good word
certainly his lessons have left many stirred
some call him exuberant for his spirit on display
such joy he exhibits nearly every day
I say he's original – no one else comes near
no one that I've ever met year after year
he's been called so many things some to insult some to uplift
I can say either way that this man is a gift
a gift that seeks to include and invite
others who haven't yet seen the light
he is a gift and I am so glad. . .
that of all the things to call him
I get to call him dad

The Cost of Hesitation

When flipping pancakes there's no time to second guess
a quick spatula will avoid a big ole mess
speed on the griddle will avoid frustration
and there will be no cost of hesitation

Vegetables on my plate gotta make em disappear
I eat em up quick so they're out of here
speed at dinner time avoids frustration
so I avoid the cost of hesitation

I know what she wants but it's not my pick
but I'll do it now and do it quick
pleasing my sweetheart avoids frustration
so I definitely avoid the cost of hesitation

Night Crawler

Footsteps quietly into the night
all alone traditionally hasn't always ended right
prone not to always make the right choice
caught up in the sounds and rhythm of my own voice
consumed with self there's little wonder
how solo episodes took me under
is tonight different? I sure hope so
cause I'm not alone anywhere I go
actually I've got a team
that is much more than it may seem
the sort of team that often transforms
lightweight showers into heavy storms
foolish jesters into valiant kings
broken tones into bellowing rings
feeble men into fierce brawlers
it turns night trippers into night crawlers

Esteemed and Honored

They wear friendship well like the truest of brothers
decades set them apart from all others
from their teens to their 70s they go ever on
neither miles nor time nor anything gone
can ever come between these two great men
time is just a number an arbitrary spin
while the earth moves these two abide
in their Father's arms safely by His side
happy to share space year after year
esteemed and honored by all those here

Home

It's where I've been for a while
but also where I long to be
I thought I'd arrived after many a mile
but I believe there's a lot more down the road for me
this is good yes but this is not it
it will indeed be the best
and not just by a little bit
but by immeasurable measures we will all find rest
our rest here is so temporary
it only comes in a small amount
but then we will lay down all that we carry
and find a wealth of rest that none can count
now all this counts too but only so much
I'm thankful for all I've received
physical provision plus my family's touch
are pointers to be believed
pointing the way where I'm headed
this all is a bit much for me
when those moments find me dreaded
Home is all I can see

Birthday Party!

It's the last week of January and already this year
an unfortunate trend has become quite clear
concerning our habits with social occasion
and we've fallen prey to a bad persuasion
I'm referring to grown-ups and their funny ways
of not partying on their birthdays
but making a big deal when somebody dies
at crowded funerals when everyone cries
I'm not saying it should be the other way around
but isn't there a better way to be found?
wouldn't it be better if they were the same?
'cause don't party and I think that's lame
to be fair I actually am the same way
but I'm about to change starting today
grown up birthday parties shall be elevated
my friends are most worthy to be celebrated
I won't wait 'til the end to speak my praise
let's all pitch in for some happy birthdays

Canvas

The first time I ever put the pen to the pad
I got the feeling like none I'd ever had
like I was alive for the very first time
the word the expression the energy the rhyme
such a blessing to have this canvas for my art
I knew this would be for me from the start
I would learn so much as my heart was stirred
that my canvas would always be for word
Written spoken filmed or recorded
these mediums saw my expressions supported
and then the best thing that ever came to be
was when I realized the best canvas is me
I am the medium for these words to be conveyed
the canvas on which His art is displayed
and this Wordsmith couldn't possibly be greater
He's the Poet I'm the poem
happily created by the Creator

One

Five days for seven classes to learn this and that
trained the same way wherever we were at
giving attention to the four
our teachers said were the core
but our core was left unaddressed
leaving us inwardly stressed
cause after all the success of getting it done
all we ever needed was the one
the one that cried out inside
the one that only we could provide
the one for which the world is in wait
the one which only we can create

Attraction

The wonder of attraction defies all circumstances
despite all obstacles attraction advances
as nothing can prevent that from getting to this
there's just no way it's gonna miss
it may take a while there may be hesitation
but you can be sure it'll reach its destination
and the fulfillment of attraction is second to none
to get to that place where you have that one
that one that brings your heart satisfaction
may you all experience this wonder of attraction

Peace or Ownership

Peace and ownership just don't get along
they're not in the same world same page
      and certainly not the same song
trying to seize them both is not unwise rather it just can't be done
both are impossible there can only be one
therefore surrender is the perfect choice
surrender to the Author adherence to His voice
letting go of ownership is difficult to say the least
but worth every bit of it in order to get peace

The Bridge

We all have a here and there's always a there
but getting across is often a scare
or at least a challenge as the trail isn't blazed
and none who have made it have crossed unfazed
for there is pain disappointment and despair along the way
and though many will have much to say
it's just you and Him getting across
so know that even in tragic loss
you are not alone for one minute
believe that and you will always be in it
I can't say when you'll get there I don't know
but let me encourage you as you go
keep putting in work don't tire of reaping
what you sow will surely be worth keeping
what you sow will be the power to send
the means to build the bridge to get you to your end

Subtle Impact

When I think of impact one thing comes to mind
a car crash that leaves a lot of wreckage behind
it's not pretty and I speak personally
the impact of a car crash is a nightmare to me
but I have experienced impact in other ways
when I consider the sum of all of my days
my calculations have an encouraging leaning
jam packed with nurturing healing and meaning
cause there's another type of impact that's greater than collision
it's one that brings together and opposes division
the sort of impact I'm referring to only needs one modifier
it only needs one adjective to take it up much higher
and it is subtle really that's what I'm talking about
subtle impact carries the power it is the straightest rout
epic impact makes the news and carries resounding note
but subtle impact is the life-jacket that keeps us all afloat
what I'm talking about are those moments
      that add up over the years
a visit a note a compliment a shoulder for shedding tears
many have them many give them my invitation is to all
sharing your subtle impact to those prone to fall
is life mercy and truth to put it mild
whether you are old or whether you are a child
we all have this in us this very good potential
this is not a small matter this could be providential
cause a God that provides for birds and trees
and calls us to love the least of these
understands the significance of subtle impact completely
in word in thought for us all may it be

Super Bowl Hijack

I've never cared for football a day in my life
if I watch it then I ask my wife
what's going on cause I do not understand
the game at all so favored in this land
as years go by and championships are done
I can never remember who has won
but now even that matters less than ever
as I certainly have something much better
cause two years ago on Super Bowl Sunday
we went to the hospital now I'm proud to say
that I do have a victory I'll never forget
this precious boy - we are all set
our Super Bowl hijack it's a permanent deal
TOUCH DOWN! this kid is for real

Begging the Hog (A Teacher's Plea)

MR GROUNDHOG! hear my plea!
please see your shadow in Tennessee!
give us the winter we're longing for
not this that leaves us wanting more
I've got about thirty teachers desperate in their ways
they're crying bitterly for some much needed snow days
we have more than two weeks allowed set aside in a stack
but if we don't use them we don't ever get em back
it's such a crime for us to waste them
It'd be so much better if we could taste them
come on snow! come on ice!
     a winter wonderland would be so right
sparkle my front porch with your beauty –
     fall on the streets tonight!

Bayboy

It's impossible to overstate
how much we enjoy
our baby our boy he's our bayboy
the laughter the smiles that he provokes
the happiness that his presence invokes
the kisses and hugs - he's such a treasure
watching him grow measure by measure
is a privilege yielding immense gratitude
he's such a blessing -
I love this little dude!

Don't Leave Me (feat. Leah Tomlinson)

Closeness comes
with a taste that's bittersweet
a dichotomy containing
victory and defeat
for past the moment of embrace
one misfortune stays
and casually we go our separate ways
I don't like it - not one bit
cause I don't ever want
the closeness to quit
snuggled up sweet
is where I want you to be
stay right here - please - don't leave me

Don't leave me
Don't go where I can't follow
I said "yes", I said "I do"
To my words let me be true
If you leave me you break them
You break us too
Don't leave me, remember all the good we can do
Not because of us, but for what He's brought us through
Truly closeness comes through victory and defeat
Stay on my team-please-don't leave me

So Many Ways

I like video games I really do
I've been playing for a while and much more than just a few
from the early 80s to 2015
these games on my TV could always be seen
I could talk about how much fun they've been
go down the road of nostalgia but then again
I'm actually thinking of something else that additionally relates
a simple fact that quite honestly aggravates
there's this thing about how video games are done
this thing about how the games are won
if you wanna beat a game I'm sad to say
that your goal can only be met one way
there's only one way to get those closing credits scrolling
only one way to be the victor controlling
earning the outcome the programmers laid out
from start to finish following their route
I just wonder in a field so loaded with imagination
could they make a game with more intriguing variation
cause I gotta wonder what the effect is on all of us gamers
when these programs program us to be repetitious samers
seeing only one possibility to a puzzle's solution
when in truth there may be more for a positive conclusion
there may be two three or seven ways to get the prize
who knows? but only trying one can't be wise
if the goal of a situation is to arrive
4+1 11-6 and 10\2 all equal 5
there are so many paths go get to where we're going
so many ways to find out what others are knowing
even lies and mistakes can lead us to what's true
just consider the diversity through which victory has come to you

The Chicken and the Bear

I always thought that if I could
get away from the bear that'd be good
cause one of these days he's gonna be
the source of of my downfall - the death of me
I hate that bear I hate him every bit
his violence is displayed hit after hit
to the point where I'm consumed every day
this bear ain't gonna get me - I've got to get away
so I'm hiding undercover laying low a bunch
he is not gonna get me! I am not gonna be his lunch!

This has worked for a little while
but deep down on the inside
evading this killer has been good
but I'm still not satisfied
cause I've gotten away
from this savage go-getter
but I can't say I'm any better
he didn't get me where I abide
but the thing is I'm empty inside
I need filling amidst all this action
escape with no nourishment
still yields no satisfaction

Now I know you may chuckle
at the next word I'm kickin'
but I've actually been filled
cause I caught me a chicken
I evaded the bear but I got the bird
and in the end that's the best word
it's what I've needed all along
both escape and eating complete my song
secure in and out loving life a bunch
the bear didn't get me and the chicken is my lunch!

The Happy Poem

This morning I woke up with burdens in my head
anxiety so early? I should stay in bed
but I got up and went about my day
and eventually I found a better way
I'll tell you what it is if you gimme a minute
you're gonna wanna know how I was able to win it
cause I bet you wake up with anxiety too
and I bet you'd like it to vanish from view
if you your mental state is leaning towards crappy
you just gotta make it happy
chocolate chip cookies fresh baked in the oven
or hot coffee with snickerdoodles is what I'm lovin'
the best magazine in my mailbox
a Superman t shirt with Batman socks
video games with friends projected on the wall
red orange leaves on trees in the fall
balloons donuts and unexpected friends
former enemies making amends
kisses and hugs from my kids – all three
my wife snuggled on the couch with me
a job well done from my excellent boss
a spicy chicken sandwich with barbecue sauce
a poem that captures everyone's imagination
steps that take way everyone's frustration
Nintendo Apple Marvel and DC
Disney Dreamworks they're all for me
writing a poem with tears on the page
then performing it live with spoken word rage
all these listed are for when you get too slappy
keep em close too my friends and always be happy

Keep Moving Forward

I know where we've been and where we're from
what we've seen and how far we've come
what we thought we were and who we are now
answering the why and figuring the how
there's a forward and a backward and the difference between the two
is that only one can happen if I am with you
there's no moving forward if I'm alone
it's only backward on my own
so you and I both of us ain't nothing better
upward and onward keep moving forward together

Casey and April

My first favorite was Raphael
the short tempered sai wielder fighting so well
and Michaelangelo has always made me smile
Chucking away with hilarious style
Donatello gets all kinds of attention
Rocking the bo staff and crazy inventions
Leonardo the solid knight completely unafraid
The master ninja leading with katana blade

These four brothers - there are none better
Defending New York against the shredder
And every other villain on multiple occasions
Killer robots and alien invasions
 I don't want to imagine my childhood without them
Even when they vanished I could never doubt them
All that being said about these brothers
There is actually still one other
And he's Actually the one I'd like to be
The one that has the most appeal to me
You see the turtles are great at saving the world
But when it's all over only Casey gets the girl
So this week lets let's give it a go
I won't be like Michaelangelo
Let's you and I fantasize for real
I'll be your Casey Jones you be my April O'Neil

Fallen

We fell in love this time of year as so many couples do
failed attempts with others brought us both back in view
it's so fantastic when I recall
     the steps that brought us home
home to each other just us alone
it was this time of year that our romance was made
it is remarkable and even more so that we've stayed
falling in love is easy but with so many distractions callin'
I thank God that He has given us the gift of staying fallen
we've thought about getting up
     in some ways we've even tried
we've fought we've cursed we've deceived we've lied
by all accounts we've overdrawn
our love banks we've been way past gone
but He Who introduced us He who started our story
has kept us together so our fall is His glory
His mercy overcomes His will is true
so thankful to have fallen so deep in love with you

What Counts

I'm crazy to say this but it is certainly true
poems aren't the most romantic thing I do
no - romance is recognizing your honey's wishes
and that's a clean room clean floor and washed dishes
to be sure when I think about it it all makes sense
but I'm not always on the right side of the fence
cause chocolate and roses are a nice display
but what if the laundry hasn't been put away?
if I do the one without the other
I may as well go live with my brother
but doing both? hey that could work!
then I wouldn't be such a jerk
my love would be received in much greater amounts
and she would be delighted - that's what counts

Hot for Teacher

Alright here's the deal there is something y'all should know
every morning when I leave for work
    I'm more than happy to go
cause I don't kiss my wife goodbye we do something better
actually we all get in the car and we leave together
we're both teachers at the same school even in the same hall
to be sure we have some difficulty
    but mostly we have a ball
some men may not like working with with their wives
they may wanna separate professional lives
but as for me it's a pretty sweet deal
happy and delighted is how I feel
as a middle school student I never had a girl
but as a middle school teacher I'm on top of the world
and in this world in Tennessee
the most beautiful lady works with me
every day is a gift cause she is the feature
never thought I would say I'm hot for teacher

Never Gets Old

Anniversaries Valentine's Day
and a few other dates are occasions to display
the affectionate attention I have for you
and you have for me we're both in view
we try to pick things we both can use
whether it's Starbucks or even a cruise
whether it's a movie or working out
or even conversation dealing with doubt
The point is for us to focus on us
and whether we bless or whether we fuss
I couldn't be more glad let it be told
that dates out with you can never get old
they just don't they're sweet as can be
just you and I out peacefully

Friend

We were friends in the first place from the very start
and that quickly evolved from my head to my heart
you became my girlfriend I beheld your beauty every day
those days were quick though
    as I asked you to be my fiancé
on top of the world? yeah for sure
a love so new so good so pure
not temporary but long enough for life
in the fullness of time I received you as my wife
emotionally physically spiritually and legally
I belonged to you and you belonged to me
could it get any better?
    is there a sequel to something this good?
in a word yes as we moved into parenthood
and that was and is a completely different story of us
with frustrations a plenty and great days glorious
since then we've added other descriptions to how we relate
travelers missionaries clients
members and teachers in the Volunteer state
but of all the titles we share
    the one I will cling to until the end
better than wife better than mom
    I treasure you most as my friend
I hope that you understand what I'm trying to say
cause our friendship means more day after day
I'm not talking about a casual friendship here
but a friendship that perseveres year after year
like Ecclesiastes 4 John 15 and Ruth 1
friendship on this level is never outdone
it was our beginning it will remain until the end
blessed that I can call you
    blessed even more that I can call you friend

Fresh Start (A Tribute to Gidget Stewart)

The end – that point where there's nothing more
finality has come and closed every door
to the house of despair while you were inside
and you can't escape no matter what you've tried
all your friends and family have said goodbye
completely alone you sit down to cry
this is no fairy tale or dark fantasy
this is your story this is your history
I wonder – if I could – in the middle of your dark
allow me to make one single little spark
allow me to elaborate on one small possibility
one small suggestion that made a difference to me
I'm not sure if you're ready – it may seem like a myth
but two words that may apply here are simply – what if
what if this is not the end as you now suppose?
what if there's a way out that I can possibly propose
what if someone can come inside into your house of despair
and show you how to navigate
      and make your way out of there?
what if there's a way to experience life again?
what if there's a second chance
      to be more than what you've been?
what if a do-over is really on the road ahead?
an avenue of courage with no room for dread
what if there is hope and healing for your heart
what if all this is true? what if there's a fresh start?

My Boat

My boat is so good it's always been the best for me
it's not perfect but it always gets me where I wanna be
I'm pretty content to stay in my boat
it's swift enough and it stays afloat
honestly I feel like it's who I've become
I am it as a whole and not just some
wait
what's that you say?
my boat is not the only way?
well I know that that's plain to see
I'm just saying my boat is the best for me
What?!
now I must disagree
a better boat for me? that can't be
there is no better boat in all creation
no craft more suitable for my transportation
my boat is stalwart tried and true
what?! you claim the better boat belongs to you?
alright I'll humor you for argument's sake
but I'm not gonna change there's too much at stake
but actually your sails look really fine
could I possibly put your sails on mine?
and while I'm at it could I have your mast too?
my boat with your sails and mast would be quite a view!
a combination of old and new could brave any weather
my boat and yours - what could be better?

A Party for Mr Voss

I'm throwing a party for Ryan Voss
all win no loss like a boss he's the sauce!
today's his birthday and he's everybody's guy
so the party level has GOT to be HIGH!
the guest list is gonna have to be crazy amazing
with characters and people with reputations blazing
like Nightwing his most favorite crime fighter of all
and Bruce Jason Tim and Damian would also get a call
and the party wouldn't be complete without an invite
to Alfred and Jim all friends of the Dark Knight
moving on from Gotham City there's more birthday bash
Green Arrow and his friends and all of team Flash
while we're inviting superheroes I'm pretty sure we can
get the Justice League Avengers X-Men and Spider-man!
the Ninja Turtles? Yeah they never get old
alright alright we can get Blue Beetle and Booster Gold
now changing worlds to something else just as cool
Link would have to come with Zelda from Hyrule
and the Mushroom Kingdom would also be good to go
Princess Peach Toad Luigi and Mario
and as for music we'll have the best choice
of listening to Dog Truck with Scruffy Bill's voice
and speaking of scruffy Han Solo would be there too
with Luke Leia and Obi-Wan also in view
but the best part of of this party for everybody's guy
would be everyone coming from the dojo Cobra Kai
Johnny Mr Silver and Sensei Kreese would meet
meet us with wonderful piñatas to beat
and do you who the piñatas would look like?
Miyagi and LaRusso riding on his bike!

beat em beat em beat em! oh what fun it will be!
the best guests the best games sure sounds good to me!
happy birthday Mr Voss thanks for all you do
enjoy today in all its glory and know we sure appreciate you

Snow Days

We already had two days anyway but now we have all five!
news that good has the punch to make the dead alive
and as for me it's better than good
I'm the happiest dude in the neighborhood!
cause I'm a teacher married to a teacher
      and we have three great kids
so today let me tell you a few of the things we did
first and foremost we stayed up late and slept in even later
played some games watched some movies
      but what was even greater
was Tuesday when all five of us bundled up to go outside
mommy and daddy pulled the sled to give the kids a ride
we don't have a hill but that was okay
we pulled em with a jump rope laughing all day
and later that night I assumed the role of tutor
by teaching them Garage Band on our computer
our 11 year old and our 8 year old too
made their own songs brand spanking new
they were immediately added to the family playlist
sure to be jammed never to be missed
so proud to see them engaged in creating
I smile cause my heart is celebrating
not just part of it but all of it every thing
days like this fill me up they make my heart sing
gratitude moves me I'm thankful in so many ways
loving life love my family
      loving everything about these snow days

Get You There

Whatever it takes - that's the bar
nothing too high nothing too far
I gotta get ya to Him He makes it right
He knows He sees because He's the Light
He's got what you need believe that
there's healing in His hands receive that
and if you don't know don't worry I got you
I couldn't care less what you think caught you
whatever's in the way whatever it is
I'll deal with it because you are His
so nothing will be able to beat
I'm gonna get you to His feet
I pity the fool that gets in my way
I'll go all night and all day
crowds will part and bridges will be made
walls will fall and bonds will be frayed
roofs will be destroyed and oceans will part
I will get you to the One who remakes your heart
do this alone? No! you can't afford
I will get you to the feet of the Lord
know that He loves you you are adored
so I will get you to the feet of the Lord
lovingkindness for you has been stored
so I will get you to the feet of the Lord
He and I are in one accord
so I will get you to the feet of the Lord

Defining Friendship (for Woody and Buzz)

There are several ironies
that they began as enemies
delusion versus jealousy neither one understanding
both with agendas incredibly demanding
the first one had his world completely arranged
the second had his mission which was completely deranged
the first one lived in fear nearly every day
the second one worried he may never get away
the first ones fears were soon realized
when his importance was soon downsized
things got real crazy with order undone
and everybody thought bad of the first one
completely estranged from everyone they knew
the only friend number one had was number two
so after they finished their personal attack
they had to rely on each other in order to get back
and in doing so their feud met its end
and beautifully they became friends
the whole process then also brought
another gift that they both got
something that originally neither one knew
but something they both needed to view
they both had ugly agendas persisting
but their friendship defined their purpose for existing
a glorious task a job of joy
their purpose was to be there for that boy

Plant the Seed

There's no telling what the end result will be
the possibilities go far beyond you and me
our perspective has limits of unfortunate severity
any predictions add up to hilarity
cause our job is just to get the thing going
and surrender the outcome to the One knowing
He does it all it is His work indeed
all we do is plant the seed

Turn on the Light
(A Tribute to Steve Brown and The Hendersonville Samaritan Association)

Dark times fall on all of us here
we hope for brevity but it could be years
for everything to get back in place
and routines to regain their pace
so now what? when feeling so defeated
and food clothes and shelter are still needed
what can be done when finances have missed the mark?
does darkness actually have to be in the dark?
the answer in a word is no
there is actually one place to go
a place modeled after its own namesake
abundant help for you to take
cause life has a way of surprising us with pain
calamity tragedy with loss to gain
but life also has the kindness of strangers
rescuing us from injury and dangers
providing transportation to a place to mend
paying the bill until the end
that's what this place is like I'm so glad I know it
their example is solid given they always show it
they show us that through dark times we can be alright
they do for us so we can pass it on
      and together we turn on the light

Positive Responsibility
(The optimist's pep talk)

It's this tenacity for positivity that fuels my optimism
between the good and I there's a magnetism
that demands we both collide and cling
but it's not just for me - I let this message ring
I know how pessimistic panic can powerfully pervade
like blistering sunshine but I've got the shade
I feel a glorious burden of responsibility
to spotlight every inch of good that I see
sometimes it's hard I'm not gonna lie
when men kill men and the innocent die
my optimism isn't naïve NO it's real
I believe good news returns what bad news can steal
bad news steals hope courage and imagination
it cripples communities cities and nations
but good news has this insane ability
to bring it all back to you and me
bring back hope courage and imagination too
good won for me it'll win for you
if we need to cry that's fine for a minute
but let's not wallow when we could win it
win a perspective so unshakeable
an attitude completely untakeable
a rise above every failure and fall
all pluses multiplying let's do this y'all!

The Next Level

Today is plenty - no further challenge necessary
no more drama needed and certainly no more scary
but frequently I find my mind getting on what's ahead
I'm focused on the next level - I dwell on the future instead
I don't admit this as a healthy way of thinking
rather it is better avoided as it leads to sinking
down in the chasm of worry and chronic anxiety
concerned about what I may or may not see
who can tell how the next level will appear?
no one at all I'm not there I'm here
and if I focus on this level I'm right where I need to be
if I master this level the next level will be given to me

Blood Sweat and Tears

Nobody told me - I knew because I was hurt
and the blood that my wounds supplied was poetry on the dirt
the pain of life - while not unique - but still filled with curses
opened the path for all these verses
and I've been doing it long enough for all these years
to realize this is also my sweat and tears
and through strains of pain joy and creation
I cry I sweat and bleed imagination

Hard Work

Nothing beats hard work enthusiasm filled with drive
such hard work is the key that makes one truly alive
to be able to see what no one else can
and problem solve with an original plan
to restore order where chaos once reigned
to understand what before could never be explained
will lead to such an ethic of action
that no other could understand the attraction
and they might say something like "wow you worked hard
your dedication never dropped guard!"
just let em think it but we both know
That that's not right it's just not so
cause hard work in its purest state
opens up every door and gate
does that sound like labor at all?
no! hard work happens in response to a call
from One higher One better One who knows
and coming from Him you know how that goes
days weeks and months putting sweat on your head
but they only feel like moments instead
hard work like that leads to changing action
that's the hard work that brings about satisfaction

Chasing Grace

Grace pulled the curtains back just enough for me to know
that there is a place I don't ever wanna go
and then grace showed me something even more dear
and exactly what that was relieved all my fear
so now I've got two frames of reference
one I'm dodging but the other is my preference
and it was grace that revealed them both to me
you could say "I once was blind but now I see"
and I'm running away a little but mostly it's a race
and I know I've already won since I'm chasing grace

Ten Thousand Hours

Ten thousand hours - go ahead and take it
you gotta practice that much if you wanna make it
to expert level in whatever you do
only the dedicated will be able to get through
cause many will begin but fewer will continue
and even fewer will finish in the treacherous venue
that separates the posers from the winners
and the snackers from those eating their dinners
it's time to feast! and the banquet is set
few are willing to try and most wanna forget
that this path is not made for all
but for those willing to knock down the wall
when no doors are anywhere near
getting over there means starting right here
ten thousand hours can't be neglected
focus your energy get yourself directed
you already know what ten thousand hours feels like
you may have to take a mental hike
back to a time when you first did
kindergarten age five you were just a kid
consider 10,000 hours later assuming you weren't delayed
you would've been 13 wrapping up the seventh grade
and that's just 7 hours a day for 180 days a year
consider what you accomplished going there to here
now think about what you could do with the eight years coming now
you could be the expert in something ima tell you how
for eight years I want you practice as if you were fighting death
give it your all as surely as you draw breath
it'll take more than a thousand hours a year
but when you get to the other side you will be here

not as a fan but as an expert standing
your advice they'll be demanding variables you'll be commanding
now suppose you're old suppose your chance has come and gone
what if you are just too near for your last breath to be drawn?
hey! listen now! that kinda thinking ain't right
you'll be alive in eight more years! why don't you start it up tonight?

Empowered (A Tribute to Kevin Lawson)

Power or authority to do something or act
if you can give this to people you will attract
more followers than your mind can begin to conceive
you'll give people the ability to believe
and understand what they have already
something for life to use on the steady
something that they've had all along
an expression a movement a gift a song
the description given to the woman or man
who moves their status from cannot to can
who move from seed to fully flowered
can be recognized as having been empowered
oh it's an amazing thing to be able to declare
that you helped someone get their idea out there
I want to support groups and individuals who make this their goal
of helping those express their soul
groups that empower people to use their gifting
are earth changing mavericks in a word uplifting
I thank God for such groups who take what could
and make it what did let's spread that good

Return to Sender

Salad bread baked potato and steak
are delicious but don't always make
me happy when eaten in such great proportions
so at 2 am my body's doing contortions
what once seemed a great culinary splendor
has violently ended in a return to sender

A Truth I've Known

There is little wonder in the fact
that a day alone does little to attract
any amount of substantial creativity
I can only go so deep introspecting me
but today I was surrounded in the usual way
by family students and co-workers as I am every day
and my mind was fluid indeed emancipated
and so restrictions fall down and these lines are created
to reveal a truth I know I've known
and that is that I'm not meant to do life alone
what a good reminder I got a day ago
down and sick slower than slow
against the backdrop of right now
at the end of today I am grateful how
a day if investing in the lives of others
friends family sisters and brothers
has all the satisfaction a day could ever hope for
so glad tomorrow I'm headed for more

Getting it Out There

"It's rooted in fear I've had since I was a kid"
if those words are yours you know what it was
      and you know what it did
it may be embarrassing a trivial situation
an inopportune moment at an inopportune location
or it could be a tragedy of grand proportions
that left your confidence with broken distortions
whatever it is can we all agree
that it has no defining properties for you and me?
I need to hear that in the worst way
cause this is something I fight with every day

Things in the Way

I have two sides that are in opposition
and their conflict manages daily fruition
my giver and my taker don't like to share
the one wants to be here the other over there
the one wants to bless the other receive
the one wants to tell the other believe
today my taker was focused on his way to live
with little to no thought on how or why to give
so it took me a bit longer to come up with this right here
some things got in the way but I got my act in gear

Sowing Goodness

I don't wanna blink 'cause I love seeing You
in every place just doing what You do
sowing goodness with more enthusiasm than I have ever seen before
only a quarter will appreciate it but you're casting seed to all four
and I reckon that's the lesson You're demonstrating for me
not worrying about how where or what the measure will be
but just doing good by scattering the seed
following Your example I'm following your lead

On the Front Row

So much of life is a big blessing
one grand gift after another with no guessing
that I could've come up with anything close
to this good on my own - no - this is the most!
I inventory all the best and I've come to learn
that all I've got would be impossible to earn
all of this is better than anything I could've planned for
sitting on the front row eager to find out what else is in
store

Seize the Goal (A tribute to Justin Swanson)

There is a tendency on the quest to be our best
for readiness to be a liability too often second guessed
cause readiness can be sufficient for the one who survives
long before completeness fully arrives
but recognizing that moment is not easily done
when to stay and when to run
it is wisdom then that must decide
whether to stay home or whether to go outside
in some ways one is really never ready to go
in those times it is comfort one cannot know
cause if sufficient preparation is made
      and there is wisdom in your soul
keep your eyes on the prize and reach out to seize the goal

The Song of My City
(A Love Poem to Washington D.C.)

Two hundred years plus this city has seen it all
war peace riots order many rise many fall
but the city remains as a beacon for many things
walking the streets I am overcome hearing the songs she sings
songs of freedom equality accomplishment and history
songs of unrest pain tragedy and solemnity
songs of hope perseverance and conviction with every breath
songs of why not and invention songs of life songs of death
the songs she sings are as varied as the children in her fold
precious in sight beautiful to behold
eternal and ageless and also ever new
this city sings for me this city sings for you
immeasurably beautiful redefining what will and what can
this city sings her song she sings her song for every man

Unknown Honor
(A Tribute to the Guard of the Tomb of the Unknown Soldier)

There's something about the dedication
devotion discipline commitment to our nation
and her children that have offered up the full measure
they did not recon their lives as a treasure
but sacrificed themselves for country and kin
now held fast in the hearts of all men
especially by those guarding the unknown
honor for honor the dead are never alone
no they receive reverent salute every hour every day
21 steps in 21 seconds with one thing to say
we honor you we honor the sacrifice you made
we honor your families and those you've left behind
      may your glory never fade

A Powerful Thought
(In Response to The United States Holocaust Memorial Museum)

My attempts to describe what I saw today would be drastically in vain
there are no words worthy enough to convey or explain
the depth of pain and tragedy I bore witness to
just reading looking and listening was all I could do
in between disgust condemnation sorrow and rage
my heart lead my mind to fully engage
and I had a thought a powerful thought in the dark
the bad guys weren't the only ones to leave their mark
there were heroes defying the wickedness of men
there were righteous pillars in the kingdom of sin
there were fighters healers and those initiating
agents of good we can now be emulating
and what sets them apart from those who did not act
is a realization it is this one fact
what you do matters - let that sink in
what you do matters - I don't mind saying it again
cause the truth is we all have a part to play
and we will all be remembered for what we do today
our acts of courage or cowardice will matter regardless of who we are
the rings ripple outward ever with no limit how far
they spread across all time far beyond the grave
since what you do matters - let's be heroes let's be brave

A Prayer for My President

You love him you hate him you hope he does what's right
you attack him you defend him you hope he supports your fight
many petition him from citizens to kings
and now I petition on his behalf to the Maker and Creator of all things

Let him lean not on his own understanding
let him delight in every Word You're commanding
let him acknowledge You before every state
and please dear Father make his paths straight
may he love justice and walk humbly before You
may he confide in and always adore you
may he be among us as one who serves all
placing himself last listening to Your call
dear God I ask for his personal protection
surround him with your angels on every direction
I ask that You put on on his marriage an abundant blessing
with love for his wife always confessing
and for his children this and every year
may his presence as their daddy be ever near
God I thank You so much for our president of these states United
may he be in Your will delighted
may he always be right though tried may he be true
may he lose himself completely and find himself in You
for the leader of this country's women and men
I ask for these things in Jesus' Name Amen!

Who is My Neighbor?

A wish to justify myself is in vain
self-serving questions won't explain
what my selfish ears want to hear
since my heart is nowhere near
the heart of the One I'm talking to
Who doesn't call me to serve some of you
but rather all of you on His earth
regardless of local value worth
He has other ideas about who is and is not
and that's why I'm an idiot caught
up in this perpetual self-serving behavior
humbled from asking "who is my neighbor?"

A Marriage Prayer (for Nolan and Alisha Crooks)

I feel my heart swell at such an occasion
holiness plus happiness make up the equation
that everyone present counts as a gift
the whole event serves to lift
up the spirits of all gathered there
so I too lift up my spirit to my Father in prayer

Father You make all things good and pure
You invented all of this for sure
this institution this relationship this day
has You all over it in every single way
so I know I can be confident with my supplication
I know You delight in our invitation
I know You delight in these two right here
so with great excitement I call to Your ear
raise them up high above the level of this earth
let their value be determined by the worth
that You have set for them as man and wife
allies under You and partners for life
put in them a desire for You above all
above each other above themselves and Father when they fall
raise em right back up with strength renewed
with focus sharpened and piety imbued
let their marriage serve as a source of truth Your Word
may it be spoken every where it can be heard
at home afar and along the way
nights of darkness and brightest day
God give them the relationship You have with Your own
holy and pure from spirit to bone
right now forevermore again and again
sanctify this marriage in Jesus' Name Amen!

Only He Could (a tribute to Wayne Brezinka)

He didn't wait to be asked he just did it
no one knew what was coming but when he hit it
they recognized it for the home run it was
and he distinguished himself from one who could to one who does
a supermodel for assertiveness and enterprise
a gift for the soul a delight to the eyes
all because he did what only he could do
only he brought such a a depth of richness to view
now people are coming in day after day
they want what he does they love his way
they love his work its comparison does not exist
it has a personality that will perpetually persist
far beyond our lives his art will remain
through the ages its echoes will explain
the richness of a heart so few knew about
no one asked him - but everyone wanted - for him to bring the inside out

Make it to Eight

A full day on my feet it's the same for her too
the dismissal bell rings but we are far from through
we both have track practice for a bit but then I'm gone
grabbing the kids on the way home - pizza time dinner's on
a few moments with dear friends more like family with common hearts
the moment is over I'm out the door time to go to martial arts
she goes to three hours of meetings no karate action
both of us just trying to make it just trying to maintain traction
we hold on to hope to the one thing we deem great
Lord, please help us make it to bedtime at eight!
we have way too much piled up on our plate
but it'll all work out if we can make it to eight!
I believe we will get there I sure hope we won't be late
I'll hang on a little bit longer very soon I'll crash at eight!

How Fast it Goes

Life is a blur at the speed of sound
everything changes the more I'm around
years become months become weeks become days
the speed of which baffles in so many ways
I wanna slow it down so I can hold on to it
but feasibility stands in my way - I can't do it
I could let this bring me down and damage my very core
but since I know how fast it goes I treasure it that much
more

Renters and Owners

Renters love em and leave em with no plan to return
owners practice wisdom as they discern
how to cultivate mature and bring out the best
renters squander but owners invest
renters pass opportunities to engage
owners plug in on every page
renters don't get it even after they're shown it
success lies with the ones who are willing to own it

Yes be Yes

I said yes but then I thought no
but then I thought I better not let this thing go
if I drop it who else is gonna do it?
integrity motivates me so I pursue it
to its own end until the whole thing is done
and regardless of the outcome I'll know I've won
not by being ahead when the time runs down
not by getting more points on the court or on the ground
I'll be a winner because I didn't cave in to stress
and among all the quitters I let my yes be yes

Give Her Dad

I know her face I see her everyday
and her smile continues to be new in every way
that is to say it doesn't get old
but it instead it is much more precious than gold
because it's her and she is a treasure
and being with her is a gift a pleasure
from her birthday to a few minutes ago
when times are quick or when they are slow
she is mine she's my daughter and wherever we go
it is a blessing to be her daddy every month of the year
knowing that I won't always be here
so each moment is that much more precious for sure
so it is so important to keep communication pure
I affirm her encourage her speak truth into her soul
I give her the tools that so she can be in control
wisdom creativity love for good hate for bad
but most of all I give her myself as her dad

Keep Courage Going

I want to make all this about me but that's destined to fail
but if I make it about you then that's more likely to sail
and if I make it about you and base my words on what you need
then we will all reap a greater benefit across the board indeed
now determining what you need is not a simple task
there are many of you so it'd be impossible to ask
I think about people I know in every state and nation
and the common ground is a need for inspiration
and specifically just so you know what inspiration is being sent
is something we all need and that is encouragement
encouragement for what? well that's up to you
but I bet we all need more courage to do
whatever it is that we know we must
rather than scrap it all and call it a bust
allow me to suggest you can
I want you to be brave you woman you man
fear timidity laziness and apathy
are not welcome in the realm where you're meant to be
you're better than that you've got this
be brave be courageous cause even if you miss
your courage will drive your tenacious persistence
and burn up all shreds of petty resistance
and you will cross that line! Oh my word what glory!
it will be yours and you will have such a story
so as to pass it on to the next one not knowing
and in turn you too will keep courage going

Have it All (a tribute to Blue Mother Tupelo)

This is as good as it gets and that's great
it's not settling but rather they've looked at their plate
and saw everything for her and him
all the best for both of them
they're content with what they have and here's how
they realize they have it all right now
sure the carrot dangles but honestly they know better
that measures taken to get it will be nothing more than a fetter
as it is realizing what they have values beyond price
they can deny competing offers and never even think twice
cause how can anyone hold a candle to
doing what you love with the one you love and they also love you!
it just works and there's no end to its delight
from early in the morning to all through the night
they're doing what they were made to do and they are good to go
ladies and gentlemen may I present - Blue Mother Tupelo

Consecrate this Dance Floor

She didn't learn to dance from just anyone
I thank God that her moves are more than just for fun
oh don't get me wrong she has a ball
but long before any boy will ever give a call
she has had a dance partner since she was three
as her father I am pleased to say it is me
and the standard has been set for love honor and respect
we move across the floor and I direct
messages of love value approval and worth
the dance floor is the world and she's the only girl on earth
I hope she gets it I hope she understands
as we step swing and glide while holding hands
I consecrate this dance floor for the rest of her days
for the rest of her life this is what stays

Observation Presentation

I'm becoming aware of holy moments all along the way
significant sanctuaries punctuating presently throughout my day
and I'm noticing things I've seen time and again
but instead with a much more profound spin
I'm hesitant to say just what they are
cause I don't want to limit them as to how far
these observations turned presentations continue to be
I'm just thrilled despite myself I can still see

Fun to Be Had

One of the best parts to being a dad
is seizing so many moments where there's fun to be had
in the car at the table or sitting on the floor
at bedtime playing video games or at the grocery store
there's fun to be had with my kids and my honey
and we dads can make nearly anything funny
take for instance this picture right here
my boy and I were waiting for the doctor to come near
and I remembered what my dad used to do
so I found the gloves and did it too
and made myself a a pretty tight hat
my boy giggled where he was at
I pulled out my phone while we were having fun
took a picture botta boom my job was done

Love Me in My Strength

I expect to be alone in my weakness
broken engagement in carnal uniqueness
is anything but attractive so yeah I get it
it hurts like crazy and I always regret it
but there is a greater pain still
that can numb my senses and eventually kill
to be alone in my strength is much more severe
to have excellence to display and for no one to be near
is worse than any alienation in my wrong
I know no one likes a bad song
so if I'm doing exactly what I should
and what I'm putting out is good
I want to be surrounded and supported
and not ignored or even purported
to be someone of ill intent
with a good facade but a wicked bent
i guess what I'm trying to say is this
we all have strengths so let's not miss
the best of all that we can do
please love me in my strength
        and together we'll get through

Look at a Picture

It usually doesn't take long for the words to start flowin'
but if for some reason my mind is slow goin'
I have an unlimited resource close within reach
and my hands listen while my eyes teach
you're probably the same way if you're a girl or a guy
cause we place so much value on what we see with the eye
I look at a picture and it tells me what to write
idea production through the sense of sight
my wife my children a sunset a tree
such pictures draw countless words out of me

You're Gonna Need a Poem

It's coming for all of us no matter who we are
no matter where we live my experience so far
seems to indicate no matter where I may be
life happens for all of you and me
and that is good and that is bad
it is cause for fear and reason to be glad
it could make you a lover or a hater
but you're gonna need a poem sooner or later
cause you're gonna fall in love eventually some day
and poetry will be the means to say what you need to say
anthemic verses will be your wings
and you will soar as your heart sings
unless it doesn't work out cause eventually you'll crash
eventually love will sour and your treasure will be trash
you'll need poetry even more then
navigating stormy seas this will be again and again
but you'll get back you'll be alright
you'll find more reasons to take delight
and you'll need a poem for every year
as life happens far and near
through weddings birthdays and graduations
you'll need a poem for celebrations
through divorces deaths and eliminations
you'll need a poem for lamentations
and on those days when there's nothing at all
you'll need a poem to jump start a stall
now there's nothing wrong with reaching for what's written
we poets love it when our words are fittin'
but if I may one thing that I would suggest
in order for you to get the best
whether it is old or whether it is new
the poem you need is the poem from you

Be You (a tribute to Jimmy Travis)

It's an age old saying but no less true
be yourself - there's only one you
critics will give you all sorts of advice
but don't pay em no mind don't even think twice
if they're suggesting that you change or depart
from the source of your creativity your heart
that's you! and really who are they?
don't even worry about the things they say
there's only One to listen to
only One can affirm or adjust what you do
and when He speaks even if you doubt it
His consistency will be all about it
and boomerang back until you understand
that He loves you and in His hand
you will find identity and truth for you to be true
He's the means and the ends for you to be you

Everyone's Cheerleader

"Hannah is everyone's cheerleader"
I'm certain you would realize this the moment you'd meet her
positivity optimism and encouragement are hers
when she's around this is what occurs
I dare you not to smile I dare you not to feel good
she's irresistible at school church and all over the neighborhood
so I'm not worried about her future next week or next year
cause anyone who works to put out that much cheer
anyone who serves as such a thermostat
will be a force for good no matter where they're at
I'm so glad that she's here with her mother her brothers and me
so glad we've got our cheerleader cheering joyfully

What Will You Make?

If you're reading this - good job - because you're among the few
who have the resources and technology to put it all in view
whatever device these words appear on may or may not be the best
but the fact that you even have access is proof enough you're blessed
so let me ask you a question since this is the case
since we have so much - what do you suppose is our place?
cause shopping posting tweeting playing and commenting sure are fun
but I wonder if that's just the surface
      and there's much more to be done?
cause I've seen these devices do even more amazing things
inspiring defending loving they project and freedom rings
to the discouraged the isolated the unaccepted and afraid
these devices serve as tools and through us wonders are made
and trust me when I say that despite the unhealthy norm
of marketing to consumers taking the world by storm
that these devices are for creating much more frequently
they are tools in capable hands to serve you and me
so now I ask you - what will you create?
what will you produce on this screen be it small or great?
a generation ago they had less no smartphones and never online
but consider they put a man on the moon in 1969
so I ask you again my repeating is no mistake
you have more power than all other eras so today
      what will you make?

Little Arms

I've been hugging people all my life
my momma my daddy my brothers my wife
I'm a bit of an expert I've been hugging for years
in every season through laughter and tears
and the remarkable thing is how hugs can still surprise
certain variations put more sparkle in my eyes
take for example the kind I'm thinking of right now
it packs all the love one hug could possibly allow
it extends the full measure of affection
it is so sweet! it is the best connection
it has no equal among the world of charms
I'm talking about the hug given from little arms

One Truth

Leave the 99 and search until the one is found
light the lamp sweep the floor
        and get the coin off the ground
wait until the lost boy returns to party with the winners
three paths to one truth - Jesus welcomes sinners

In the Meantime

Friday night happened and Sunday's on the way
but what do you do in the meantime what do you do today?
what do you do when all your hopes are dashed
against the rocks of reality where optimism is smashed
and the Man you placed all trust in is now dead
no good news no answers just confusing questions instead
locked in a low lit room feeling incomparably vexed
disappointment upon disappointment what could possibly
come next?

Nailed to the Cross

The list gets longer every time I turn around
opening my big mouth when I shouldn't make a sound
being quiet when I should stand up and speak
the list says I'm a liar a cheater a deceiver a sneak
the list stands between me and my family and friends
creating confusion and ridiculous spins
like we're enemies even though we're not
could be moving on but we're still caught
caught in a trap that won't cease to persist
all because of this stupid list
I hate it I hate it more than I can say
it makes me see night while it's still day
I hate it I do but I know Who hates it more
I know Who it hurts deep down to the core
I know who realizes the magnitude of loss
I thank God this was the list that was nailed to the cross

So it is finished I am free indeed I live
we will be with Him in paradise cause He said Father forgive
what stands between my God and I?
what standard of justice convicts me to die?
what accusation stands against the Lord's anointed?
who will change the appointment of he whom God has appointed?
the list?! I don't think so!
not only is it gone but it is God that made it go
He doesn't even remember it it is nothing in His mind
the list is no where in His presence you cannot possibly find
if you search for it chalk it up to a joyful loss
my brothers my sisters the list was nailed to the cross

Walk in forgiveness walk anew
the list no longer has any weight on you
it is gone forever rejoice in emancipation
You are ransomed forever to live in celebration
your list my list mark it off as your greatest loss
the list - forever - is nailed to the cross

Walking in Her Gifting (for Tia Mitchell)

Encouraged to encourage blessed to bless
inspired to inspire progressed to progress
she gives because it was given to her
gifted to gift greatness will occur
in the hearts and minds present to her measure
witness is borne to invaluable treasure
that's what she is gives and creates
taking her audience to the pearly gates
they know they've encountered God most high
and there are smiles snaps and amens some laugh some cry
all respond to the message downpour showered
she brings His reign and we are all empowered
to think do and in fact be great
these blessings are so big we need a second plate
a second net it reminds me of the Lord
the catch went crazy and the fish were overboard
this is what it's like when we respond to His choice
when we lay down our will and follow His voice
when we put away our silly suggestions
      and submit to his plan
no weapon formed can prosper no dark force no man
can stand against her or us engaged so uplifting
I thank God for my sister walking in her gifting

An Idiot's Observation

Great happiness and satisfaction can be found
in a continually clean room
      where all your stuff is off the ground
clothes hung books put up and a bed nicely made
such organization makes the absolute best grade
they say that genius is recognized by domestic disarray
but they are lying cause it's just not that way
genius is not without pragmatic practice
not done in one big swoop the matter of the fact is
a little every day is really much more fun
than letting it build into a mountain
      and never getting it done
I'm not gonna say which one I know about
but if you look at the picture above
      I've left little room for doubt

Ideas are for Sharing

Did you ever have an idea without really knowing
whether or not it was really flowing?
like maybe it's good maybe it's bad
but you wouldn't know quite what you had
until you went ahead and put it out there
put yourself on the line to go ahead and share

You'll never know without the risk to take
never know the good you'll make
unless you try and just go for it
turn it lose don't you dare store it
if it's bad you gotta get it gone
out of your head - don't turn turn that junk on
and if it's good it'll blossom into a mighty tree
and bless all that come by - try it you'll see
its branches will shade the weary from the scorching sun
it's fruit will feed those who always had none
for what you put out was good they were waiting
and now the nations are celebrating
your potential realized your purpose discovered
the risk revealed your brilliance uncovered
your enemies now your friends with support declaring
what are you waiting for? ideas are for sharing

Check-in

Three days in a row of non-stop fun
two more to go - I've only finished one
live spoken word just now on the stage
some verses memorized some off the page
alternating with my sister for the hometown crowd
her return to the mic and I'm so proud
that I could be there and see her come vividly alive
through word expressed and I find that I've
been been blessed beyond by all this word
but it's just Wednesday so this is a third
of all that's gonna happen this week
tomorrow holds more opportunity to seek
seek out a student who can be the best
headed down to Murfreesboro for a science quest
taking my kids to see what they've created
I hope it goes well and they are celebrated
but for now I'm swimming all in my head
Good night y'all I'm going to bed

Leading the Way

It is such a good feeling it's the good kind of pride
that I feel for these students deep down inside
say what you want about this generation
but I've seen what they can do and I'm filled with elation
they explore create invent and discover
they learn think solve and uncover
secrets that the grownups are baffled by
they don't accept things as they are they wanna know why
I would say I'm looking forward to the future but I'm not
on the contrary I have a much more encouraging thought
not waiting for the future they're doing it today
these kids are the ones that are leading the way

Show

It's time - so I get everything ready
set list made rhymes rehearsed everything is steady
I walk through the front door ready to go
it's Friday night and I've got a show
I do what I do and it goes pretty well
everyone had fun as far as I can tell
but there's something even better that I see
it's not my show but what was shown to me
cause I came with my sweetheart my princess and little guy
three treasures I watch from the stage with my eye
my parents came too to hear my report
their encouragement is life as is their support
I had several cousins to come tonight
they also performed and it was outta sight!
and several co-workers came by too
their presence was a most beautiful view
it really meant a lot that they came to hear
what I had to say now I'm in high gear
not because of my show but because of who I see
thank you for reminding the show's not about me

Getting it Together
(a tribute to my parents on their 45th anniversary)

My parent's love story is a good one for sure
since 1970 their status has endured
through thick and thin high and low
and for forty-five years now they've managed to grow
to a state worthy of imitation
imperfect but worthy of emulation
and it gives me so much hope so much confidence
staying together makes so much sense
no it's not easy and that's not even the point
cause it's no surprise when we disappoint
and I know that mom and dad have done it plenty
but excuses for quitting? they don't have any
because they never quit
despite failures despite disappointments despite all of it
they persevered through it all
      they grabbed a hold and held on
that's what I'll be holding on to long after their gone
theirs will be the stuff of legend for my brothers and me
our parents modeled exactly how it's supposed to be
getting it wrong getting it right but getting it together
defying performance and all kinds of weather
such an example is the most ideal view
getting it together - that's what we'll do

It's Like Breathing (a tribute to Crystal Jones)

We know who we are we know what we're supposed to be doing
but sometimes life is an obstacle to our higher pursuing
sometimes we forget or maybe just put on hold
our passion our calling our spark but thank God it is never sold
it is never lost indeed it never goes away
to quote a friend "it's like breathing" so it's definitely here to stay
we may suppose it's not real or there are other things we lack
but the thing - the real thing - always boomerangs right back
circumstances have a way of drawing these things out
things and people have a way of eliminating every doubt
because it is like breathing it's exactly what we're supposed to do
it wouldn't be right to stop and anyone who would ask you to
has no idea who you really are
so you just keep on breathing and there's no telling how far
you will go within yourself within others and most of all within Him
keep in mind the deepest breaths are reserved for the deepest swim
let that map the way for what you do now
only you and the Father will know how far and how
you just keep breathing and let Him provide the air
you just keep breathing and He will meet every care

Always More

There's always more there's always more
no one has seen all that's in store
for any subject and any category
no one can close the book on the story
not all has been spoken or heard
more remains hidden more remains unstirred
every time I arrive at any concrete conclusion
I realize later the depth of my delusion
and how shortsighted my perceptions had become
and my so-called discoveries just make me sound dumb
my hasty wrap ups leave too much out
so now I endeavor to proceed with more doubt
in what I've heard thought or seen
in what people do versus what they actually mean
cause there's always more there's always more
no one has seen all that's in store

Send Your Words

The power of life and death is contained in speech
whether written or spoken its potential to reach
is nothing less than infinite for real
so let's use them to love and to heal
because we all felt those that never did
whether grown up or still a kid
the pain remains indefinitely
and wounds become scars on you and on me
words - they're so strong they go so deep
it's a lie when they say that talk is cheap
cause so-called cheap talk hurts a lot
unfulfilled promises with action not
being accompanied with by the speaker
are cancerous which leave the listener weaker
and I'm not even describing something major
this is something that occurs in everyday behavior
the mean of negative communication
infests our culture with casual intimidation
send your words like water to a parched population
send your words for comfort and sweet consolation
send your words to defend the defenseless and voiceless
send your words to lead the way
      for the trapped who feel choiceless
words are support and strength they restore and uplift
precious beyond description words are a gift

Draw It Out

If I give it to em nobody will learn
so I practice patience this is their turn
this is their time to shine in the sun
and besides I'm not the only one
who can draw out what's already there
life has a way of directing what they declare
so I'm a part of many more who will attempt to reach
these brilliant young minds that we teachers teach
so glad I'm not their only chance
I'm not the only adult promoting their advance
it is encouraging when I think of it that way
there's no telling how far past today
these students will escalate across this nation
this world even I could offer up my estimation
but I'm sure the reality is even better it's true
looking forward to what these students will do
and not only that but what they're doing
no waiting on the future for what they're pursuing
it is now it is strong and it crushes every doubt
so blessed beyond that I get to be here to draw it out

Strong Force (the musings of a Star Wars dad)

By the time I was 9 in the third grade
the original trilogy had already been made
and unfortunately I was too young to go
but early elementary saw me catching up on video
and did I love it! Oh my word I did!
cereal cartoons action figures such wonders for a kid
I had the Ewok village Jabba the Hut
      and a storm trooper's speeder bike
a long time ago in a galaxy far far away this stuff is totally what I like
and it stepped out for a minute for a moment to remain unseen
but in 1997 it was time for them to return to the big screen
I have fond memories sitting in the theater feeling very alive
in my early 20s I felt like a kid watching episode five
it wasn't too much later that the prequels came
some of it was good but some of it was lame
but the coolest thing that overshadowed the bad
was in 2003 when I became a dad
and then before long a few years later
I got to experience something even greater
the happiness unparalleled never will be done
sharing Star Wars with my daughter and my son
and since then there's been everything a plenty
the supply has been anything but skinny
and now AND NOW we reside in geek heaven
in eager anticipation for episode VII
December can't get here fast enough
cause my whole family loves this stuff
2015 so glad they're making
so ready for Star Wars: The Force Awakens

Guacamole is Delicious

Guacamole is delicious but not everyone agrees
some would rather pass but I'll take more if you please
the fact that you may or may not like it
      makes no difference to me
if guacamole is around then it's the best place to be
it's a party if there's guacamole there
on chips on burgers in burritos I'll eat it anywhere

Room For Surprise

Leave room for surprise to such a degree
that you could be caught off guard frequently
because guardedness and careful preparation
are the allies of expectation
and expectation is the enemy of surprise
complete predictability before your eyes
but when we lose expectation
      the whole world is full of wonder
surprise is around over and under
take for example the weeds seen here
who would've thought they could appear
with such presentation of beauty outside
with little to no effort they barely tried
but someone with a camera and two keen eyes
got down and found us all a surprise
I bet she didn't expect to behold such a view

she got a surprise what about you?

Model Teacher (a tribute to Rashad Rayford)

Demonstration with instruction and instruction with demonstration
he models what he teaches giving such an education
to his students which will never spoil or fade
but with foundational integrity such lessons are made
so that these lessons they won't soon be forgettin'
because these lessons are much more
      than just the words he's spittin'
they're more than just words on the mic that sound fresh
these words aren't just words - these words have flesh
and bones and muscle geared to move with action
the positivity plus performance
      promotes community attraction
and the people have been gathering
      by the thousands every year
it's true that they want to listen they definitely wanna hear
but that's not the only benefit they get from this great man
in addition to being inspired they find they also can
do what he does they can practice what he's preaching
that's what I'm talking about his ability for reaching
defies death in some instances for real
his words have been known to comfort and heal
that's why I wanna do what he is doing
that's why I wanna be in the same way pursuing
the path that helps others make the choice
of finding and using the sound of their voice
and I know I can't do it unless I model it too
so in the same fashion I present to all of you
the example set by this great man
if he if I if you we all can

What's your Story?

So often the stories that are better to tell
have to do with those times we weren't doing so well
and we made mistakes which lead to consequences
as we were on both sides of the fences
or maybe we abandoned any hope of being cleaner
and walked in foreign countries
      seeking grass that was greener
only to find it did not exist
and now we're in a place where the point has been missed
everyone has a story of this kind
where folly leads us to lose our mind
and somehow somehow we walk away
to find God running full on down the drive way
this is everyone! I'm telling y'all what
we all have had life kick us square in the butt
and gone head over heels with absolutely no clue
I can honestly say this is me this is you
but it's so hard to talk about it we don't wanna look bad
back then we thought it would all end up glad
and embarrassment followed when it did not
so talking about it puts us in a knot
we'd rather sit back relax and deny
while we're sipping on a soda and telling a lie
or ten or a hundred or a thousand or more
but dishonesty renders no conclusion to war
if there is to be any remedy
for the junk that weighs down the past of you and me
we must find a way to get our story out there
it won't be easy when we endeavor to bare
the very thing that robs us of glory
but let's get started - what's your story?

The Weird Al Poem

Go silver go gold go platinum get a Grammy
take your band on the road from LA to Miami
be on Fallon, Colbert, Kimmel
      and perform at the Super Bowl
cross every achievement off the list meet every goal
and there is still one more thing left to be done
one more mark of success
      before you ride off in the setting sun
and it's not an audience with the pope
      the president or any kings
movie soundtracks or a duet while your idol sings
it's not playing underwater or orbiting outer space
it's not actually something you can do
      nope it's not your place
the measure of success for artists in pop
and country and rock and even hip hop
is not even whether or not you're true
but rather when Weird Al makes fun of you
and when this happens there will be hilarity
the satisfaction you've been covered by the king of parody
you'll be among those kicked back relaxin
like Madonna Billy Joel and even Michael Jackson
MC Hammer Nirvana Milli Vanilli and Eminem
Taylor Swift Pharrell Robin Thicke and all of them
the highest form of flattery is his imitation
having his voice sing your song on a hit radio station
is the way to fame and glory of a kind that will ever stick
you'll know you have arrived
      when you're covered by Weird Al Yankovic

Not Alone

Intelligence is the enemy of self-reliance
going solo snubbing teamwork compliance
doesn't work for me as I've come to learn
that going alone when it's my turn
to do anything that I want to amount
I'm gonna need help if it's gonna count
reaching out is humbling in terms of delegating
but messing up solo is downright humiliating
so I'll take the former time and again
getting help from my bros so I can win
sounds much better than thinking I can do it on my own
I know what happens when I go it alone
and it's not good I can tell you that
so in order to be successful wherever I'm at
I send a little message to my bros on the phone
in prayer they hold me up and I'm not alone

This Great Day

What a good day from sunrise to sunset
of a kind that I won't soon forget
blessings poured out from beginning to end
great family great work a great day with great friends

This morning waking up right next to
the splendor of a most fantastic view
my beautiful wife my partner and queen
blessed beyond through every scene
and then on to meet with my guys
we get together and that way we are wise
wiser than the thoughts we have in isolation
but forsaking such realities we put red lights on temptation
and green lights go on righteousness
representing manhood we're a beautiful mess
then on to work where I'm totally in my zone
analyzing poetry - this lesson I own
I got observed at a great time by my coordinator
and when we follow up on my lesson later
I'm not worried about my marks be it five or one
she loves those students and she's helping me get it done
then right after school I was able to see
a friend who seriously inspires me
her story is God blessed God centered and God moved
the word of her testimony is His glory proved
next on the agenda was also a major winner
friends for H'ville Samaritan dinner

such excellent examples were recognized and awarded
their deeds honored and their stories reported
so glad to be be there overwhelmed to be in it
and they even let me do poetry for a minute
so now we're home and feeling great
with DLC for Mario Kart 8
downloading in the background while I reflect
about this great day with gratitude direct
to the One who gives gives and gives more
than I could ever begin to be thankful enough for
but that won't stop me from at least trying
what a great day there's no denying
God thank You for taking me from start to end
when I wake up tomorrow let's do it again!

Richer Find

Half the time I have no clue
I'll think I know but when I go and do
I find that the thing wasn't the thing at all
and disappointment has me making a call
to dial in what I think but I'm still not right
it'd be cool I guess I'd like to if I might
call it get it enjoy it and be blessed
I don't know I don't know what's best
He does He knows He's got all the right plans
no guessing involved when it's coming from His hands
tonight stands in testimony that I definitely don't know
my plans thoughts and ideas
      may or may not be the way to go
but if I wait on Him and see what He's got in mind
experience proves it a far more richer find

Daddy

Put a big ole daddy right in the middle
of two great kids who are fairly little
and it doesn't matter where we go
we can get there fast or take it slow
either way no matter how it's done
it's gonna be a ton of fun
when daddy's in the middle one thing is true
surrounded by those kids he becomes one too

Tall Tale Teller (in tribute to Minton Sparks)

On the shoulders of so many she makes her stand today
she towers to such a height that none of us can look away
because the beauty in the familiar significance we see
reminds us of people and places where we used to be
perhaps a different town perhaps a different name
but her stories serve to remind us
     that we are mostly the same
and though she acknowledges dysfunction and pain
bullies and bad guys driving us insane
it yields encouragement to just to think
and remember with a smile and a wink
or perhaps a tear silently shed
at the depth of the the things she just said
and what she's lived and what she sings
it's more than just what one moment brings
more than these words in metered rhyme
more than even just her lifetime
but the living and the dead speak through her verses
and through tales of humor of blessings of curses
a richness is discovered in the wonder that is shown
villains and cheaters though we be we are never alone

It's There

If you bar graphed the statements of my first eleven years
you would notice one sentence raised up higher
you can probably guess what it is
      if you understand one thing
from the time I was born until I was a sixth grader
I lived in nine different cities on both sides of the 48 and 1 in the Pacific Ocean
it's safe to say my communication
      was monopolized by introductions
I was the new kid six times in elementary school
and not even now have I grasped
      the fullness of the impact of growing up that way
I just know that my diverse experience created exceptionalities which created strengths which created weaknesses which created me
so now I come to you with more than mere introductions
somewhere along the way I learned something better
I learned that people are less interested in who I am but much more in themselves
everyone is fighting a hard battle
and so many don't know who they are
I travel with reminders to thwart forgetfulness
because the only thing that's worse than believing you're bad is not believing you're good
I'm here to tell you that you're good because that is how you were made
you are good regardless of what you've done
how you appear or what you feel
the goodness in you wasn't put there by you so getting rid of it is not something you can do
I can tell you that it may be buried deep and on some level it may not have come out in a long time
but it's there
oh is it ever

Still Say Yes

No matter how many times you've said "no"
you can still say yes
the path back home is a long way
      and it's true you've made a mess
but so many have come back
      indeed who were worse off than you
and home is still beyond the horizon just barely beyond
your view
don't worry about today - today won't quite get it done
say "yes" now plus a thousand times
      all journeys begin with step one

I Love My Brothers

I cannot begin to tell you how energized I feel
when us four boys get together for real
I think this is how it should be always
we should be neighbors for all of our days
but we live in two different states and four different cities
such limits has us creating ditties
when we could be composing symphonies
holding the world hostage to beautiful melodies
this is all metaphorical of course we don't all make music
but a T bro headquarters? I feel like we could use it
do you realize how long it's been
      since we lived in the same town?
decades have passed since we had such common ground
is there some mystery here waiting to be undone?
truth be known we haven't shared city limits since 1991
more than 20 years have come and gone since then
and when I think about it like this it seems like sin
nothing right about it the whole thing makes me sad
for us to be so separated it just feels bad
I don't mean to whine but it does help to admit
that I don't like the miles between us not one bit
I feel like I'm more myself when we're all together
I feel like life is richer I feel like life is better
I love these men and this will ever be
I love my brothers they mean the world to me

Press the Button

I press the button every day
and I've been doing it for a while
I press the button because I enjoy it
and I feel like I'm pretty good at it too
when I press the button I plug into my purpose
I plug into who I was made to be
I was made to be that guy who can press the button
I don't know though
maybe there's more to it
I've been noticing something else that's kinda like pressing the button
but it's different at the same time
so here recently I press the button pull the lever and that seems to work pretty well
it's lead me to a place of gratitude and the only way I figured out how to pull the lever was to press the button
so now I'm wondering
I'm wondering what else I'm capable of
I'm wondering what else I can add to press the button pull the lever
cause really that can't be it
oh boy! I've got if!
I can turn the wheel!
Yes!
I can now press the button pull the lever and turn the wheel
it sure feels good to press the button pull the lever and turn the wheel
I can't believe all I ever used to do was simply press the button
but that's where I started that's where I got it going
I thank God for those days of press the button
and I thank Him even more for press the button pull the lever turn the wheel

but I wonder and you probably do too
Hey!
I bet you I could start the pump
I know I know it's a lot but seriously consider it!
press the button
pull the lever
turn the wheel
start the pump
YEAH!
press the button
pull the lever
turn the wheel
start the pump

Hmmm, I wonder if I could do one more

Step Out that Door (Hawkeye's Pep Talk)

The past was the past but right now is the present
and what lies before you is pure opportunity
stay where you are and no one will judge you
but if you step out that door you're one of us
if you step out that door you hold your head high
and release your cry of righteous energy
letting the bad guys know who you are now
you don't belong to them anymore
your gifts aren't for revenge
but instead to avenge
rescue and make right in a word save
the fierce beauty of your goodness will light the way
for others who are arriving at similar conclusions
your power their power our power is here
sound the cry what it's for
make war like a hero when you step out that door

The Sun's Beauty

The past can be explosive - a terrifying fright
the stuff from last month last week
    and and especially last night
distance is required for a proper perception
the farther your position the truer your conception
it takes a long time for the scary stuff to be understood
and a longer time still for it to be recognized as good
it's kinda like the sun you see every day
it's beauty is unmistakable as you go about your way
but if you were to see it up close that'd be really bad
it wouldn't help at all and you wouldn't be very glad
but as it is the sun's beauty is understood
    because of its location
93 million miles away at the center of our station
we cannot view it as it is but only as it was
the same is true for pain and the reason is because
the moment offers only so much grace
but a big step back puts it all in place

Tremendous Blessing
(a tribute to Courtney Nichols)

A thread of kindness consistently runs through
the length of her story for all to view
beginning with a teacher who provided every day
care and the wisdom to recognize a different way
so that that pain could be recognized as just that - pain
and steps could be taken and doctors could explain
what in the world was going on
a condition a disease that would never be gone
such a diagnosis for one so young
a hindrance to confidence with expectations stung
time went on and year after year
it always seemed like a cure was so near
but her experience would consistently teach
that such a cure would remain out of reach
but there was one man who appeared on her screen
that was unlike any she'd ever met or seen
who demonstrated sensitivity wisdom and great resolve
with a mind to address and a will to solve
the unfortunate complexities
      that others couldn't understand
so she became his wife and he became her man
what a companion to have for the next major turn
in the next moment she would learn
that her disease had taken a major toll
and a transplant would necessary to make the goal
of staying alive to fight on longer
and managing variables in order to stay stronger
so the steps were taken in all necessary ways
and provision happened in eleven days
the timing couldn't have been more on point
when it is God's will you can bet He will anoint

the situation as challenge with His blessing
He sees He knows there's no point in stressing
over what He did and still does control
such reminders build up the richness of my soul
with a new lease on life there was something else too
another idea had come into view
which included the two becoming three
and let me tell you
     God knew already how that was gonna be
He provided in a way only He could
which demonstrated His authority and never ending good
and like the transplant there was ever so much more
blessing upon upon blessing from His infinite store
so that best case scenarios seem like disappointments
next to the provision of His holy appointments
the pain misunderstood misdiagnosed
     and understandably stressing
has been an avenue of tremendous blessing
from start to finish this has been the case
life brought pain but God brought grace

Stay on Task

I say yes but I quickly think no
like it's not really the direction I wanted to go
so I flounder procrastinate and put it off another date
hoping in the end that I'll actually be too late
but someone calls me on it at Your invitation
not a harsh word mind you but it did end my hesitation
so I got up got on got out and went
I did my doing and did not relent
so glad I have friends who are willing to ask
me to keep my word and stay on task

Explosive Gratitude

Perspective is everything - how you take it in
the minute can be massive if you take it for a spin
when most folks are just taking their turn
they're unimpressed but you could learn
that there is more much more at stake
and it really is authentic not a bit of it is fake
mostly children understand how this takes place
the simplest pleasures light up their face
so that happiness is around anywhere
around any corner you can hear them declare
their excitement for what has just been going on
the moment is short and it is quickly gone
because another one is coming in just a minute
their explosive gratitude is beautiful right there in it
it's as if the moon so glorious in its view
was chosen just by God and hung there just for you

God Gave Us Goosebumps

On mountaintops
in front of oceans
around deep thinkers
before musicians
and hearing truth spoken with conviction
my brain interacts with my spirit and I know my senses were meant to
hear what I heard
see what I saw
and experience what I felt
not only does my mind react
my body does too
involuntarily I might add
it's just my natural programming
which leads me to think some pretty fantastic things
consider this if you will
suppose you hear the most beautiful magnificent song you can possibly imagine
well among other bio-emotional reactions you're probably gonna get goosebumps
and I suppose if we had the right magnifying glass we would see some interesting things
some amazing things
you see I'm convinced that we're wired for praise
and in those moments where words fail I suspect God gave us goosebumps
goosebumps are what we get when something is so awesome that the very suit that contains our soul dances in response
and this is not a pretty dance
oh no
this is a wild-eyed top of your lungs butt naked passionate lover's holler across the Grand Canyon dance

it's a get out of the way I just got back and I haven't seen my wife in 10 months dance
it's a my team just won the girl said yes my enemy is now family dance
this is what it means when we have goosebumps
the wordless outcry to the movement of the soul

Three Years to Change

Three years to change the world can it be done?
distractions abound from tuning out to too much fun
but work beckons in varying degrees
and trust me - she is not here to people please
true she doesn't mind having fun provided it fits within
the framework for success an appropriate means to an end
and that end comes up so fast every year
each group rotates right through right here
and sometimes it seems like it is way too fast
like we need another way to try and make it last
but it is folly to wish for such things
for wisdom is content with what reality brings
and the truth is three years is enough
but the prerequisites for success are tougher than tough
in fact it's gonna take all we've got
every word action idea and thought
late nights early mornings and all over again
many defeats before a single win
but that win will come and you will see
sometimes subtle sometimes obvious
      but straight to you and me
no we don't do this in isolation
every man for himself isn't our narration
but all for one and one for all
I've got your back if you should fall
and I know you've got mine so glad you do
we're a team so together we'll make it through
arm in arm side by side leaving behind all fears
ready to change the world - all it takes is three years

Having a Blast

These are my people unmistakably extraordinary
beautiful and amazing there's a richness we always carry
from early in the morning 'til the last thing we do
it's the best thing just to be with my few
everybody says these days are way too fast
so while our family's young we're gonna have a blast
taking joy down the road it's so good to know
we ride together wherever we go

Such Comfort

We all need comfort from the moment we arrive
crying out - mercy! - brand new and alive
the first five minutes set a lifetime's tone
drawing near to the one we call our own
and more importantly she calls us the same
and there is love when she calls - the sound of my name
when she wants my attention is unlike any other I know
her sound her touch her appearance
      she is the soil in which we grow
it's the comfort she provided that nourished us root to leaf
it's her constant comfort that brought forth solace and relief
in times of good and times of bad
it was she who made us glad
maintaining a level like no other
comfort such comfort from the hand of our mother

Redefine the Measure
(in tribute to Raichon Morand)

Stop me
I dare you
I'd like to see you try
tell me I can't and I will look you square in the eye
and tell you that can't don't live here it's just that simple
my optimism won't let can't enter this temple
yes - my body is broken - so what?
pity will not govern my response
        puny thinking didn't make the cut
woe is me is not of this team
give up and give in have been ripped at the seam
by a will set on total victory
complete for us and certain for me
to the point where it's everywhere I go
I was supposed to wallow around and say no
but I say heck yeah to all of it cause life is a treasure
and because I say yes I redefine the measure
the measure had limits and it wasn't for me
but my existence moves them onward - just as I'm sure they should be
I'm happy to move them onward they don't need to stay
but with improving and evolving we'll see the better way

Back in Black

It doesn't take a moment before I'm even out of bed
and in my mind I'm already in red
overdrawn by the weight of the crap left in my brain
unchecked unrecognized it would leave me insane
but my brothers who love me a bushel and a peck
help me recognize what's going on so it's all kept in check
and believe me it's the truth when I say
that it's not just one text at the start of the day
but an intentional effort to reach out again and again
show me the man who can alone can tame his sin
the power of evil is broken by the bonds of fellowship
brother to brother to brother we will stand and not trip
they're praying for me now I know they've got my back
rolling out in confidence no more red I'm back in black

Tuesday Friday

Any other Tuesday we would've watched TV
after supper it's fun for my family and me
Barry Allen with his powers taking down rates of crime
it's pretty much our favorite show we have a fun time
but tonight was better it was really good I'd say
tonight was a Friday masquerading as a Tuesday
old friends were over and it's easy to admit
that I loved every moment every single bit
we were able to hang with them - our kids felt the same
the night sped by as usual but I was so glad they came
friends like these are treasures absolutely
so we penciled plans real soon to get together resolutely
what a blessing they are so good in every way
love and peace to all my friends
       who make a Tuesday feel like a Friday

Time Bomb Ticking

I'm playing with fire I'm a time bomb ticking
these aren't exactly the circumstances I'd be picking
but they picked me for better or for worse
it doesn't seem like a blessing but much more a curse
you see my allergies managed to find me tonight
now I'm wheezing hacking and not feeling quite right
so I took some Benadryl a few minutes ago
and now I'm starting to go real slow
to the point where I may fall asleep at any time
and be unable to finish this rhyme
I trust you'll understand - that I'm not being cheap
but I hope to finish this before I fall asleeeee

Worth Remembering

I took a lot of people's pictures today
    and that is a good thing
all of them are worth remembering for all the joy they bring
students and teachers acquaintances and friends
these are the means to all my to my happy ends
you are my exclamation marks in a world of dots
you are my bubbles in a world of spots
and I wouldn't trade a one of you nope not a single one
your value your inherent value will never never be done
I realize that very soon many of you are going away
on to bigger important things
    so it's not possible for you to stay
you will be missed these years have not been spent in vain
your absence will be noticed and knowing you has been a
great gain
we send you in strength power knowledge and truth
the experience of wisdom and the energy of youth
take what you have be ready to tell
clothe yourselves with honor and wear it well

Sweetly Resting

It comes as no surprise that every now and then
our two year old is so upset it is a desperate state he's in
until we pick him up rub his back and kiss him on his head
and set him down resting sweetly in his bed

It is still no surprise that on some days and nights
our eight year old's imagination is raised to anxious heights
until we pick her up rub her back and kiss her on her head
and set her down sweetly resting in her bed

It is not really a great big surprise
when our eleven year old carries fear behind his eyes
until we pick him up rub his back and kiss him on his head
and set him down sweetly resting in her bed.

For there is no age I can think of
who doesn't need a little extra love
the point of all this is just to say
that we all need it in more than one way
we are little we are sweet we are precious in His sight
so glad He watches over and protects me through the night

The Gospel According to Mom

I'm not saying this was the plan I honestly don't think it was
plans are great don't get me wrong but I feel this way because
a thoughtful observation into my family's history helps to clarify
significant trends and important facts - hang on -
      I'll tell you why

Mom likes to write a bit but it comes in bits and pieces
if she wrote all the stories she's actually a part of
      her writing would be ceaseless
unfortunately she errs on the side of not writing nearly enough
easy for me to say since I write a ton of stuff
here recently though I've been thinking that my criticism is
grossly misplaced
she need not write a single thing
      she's given the world more than a taste
imitating her Savior Who wrote even less
what she gives the world is much more to bless
her four sons are the books that tell her story
the lives we live testify to the glory
more than an article a book or any dot com
four brothers are the gospel according to Mom
sent our separate ways with audiences unique
four completely different industries still we seek
to spread the influence of the Kingdom through the lives we live
our years are the pages it's an honor to give
witness to the One Who gave us her
in the years to come who knows what will occur?
unlimited uninhibited with a rock solid foundation
living our lives responding in blessed exclamation
we are her biography that will never spoil nor fade
her letter to the world fearfully and wonderfully made

Solid Gold (a tribute to Gabby Shrum)

One mom
one dad
two babies
three days
and they realized not all was up to speed
their son was doing well but their daughter had an unmet need
so the boy went home but the girl did not
to another hospital to see what was caught
to see what was wrong and what they could do
to put understanding back into view
one week later they were able to realize
and the journey at that time just to stabilize
was two more weeks of working and learning
brand new parents praying and yearning
for this precious baby girl in whom they were delighting
all ready to do it all all ready for the fighting
of the most noble campaign they would ever know
at last the time came for them all to go
home with feeding tubes instructions and care
and a normal life that was neither here nor there
but this was their normal this was their beginning
and refusing self-pity I'd say they were winning
a year later they didn't take it lying down
they went walking to stand with others in town
seven years later I sit with them impressed
an outsiders look I would never have guessed
what they had been through all these years
overcome challenges overcome misunderstandings
      overcome fears
such a great example of fighting effort so bold
standing set apart undaunted they are all four solid gold

Brothers Right Here

I've seen the rage and felt the fear of brothers
locked in conflict hating one another
and it's the scariest stuff I've ever seen
to this day I remember what I witnessed as a teen
you all know what it's like to see two people you love
at each other toe to toe with no gloves
for absorbing the shock you just pray that they miss
we know all that but what do you do with this
what can be done with these brothers right here?
locked in the wonder of how the other appears
affection immeasurable between the two
such love such acceptance in a single view
and this is not staged! this is not a fake
this is not a moment I was able to make
but real harmony real peace sublime
and I just happened to be there at the right time
so what do you do with brothers so devoted you could cry?
anything you want. The limit is the sky.

We are Teachers

Few things are more appropriate to sum up what we do
than tug-o-war cause working together
     is the only way we get through
we pull against students parents
     each other and administrators
custodians nurses secretaries and coordinators
and sometimes we pull against opponents unseen
and not knowing who we're against makes everybody mean
but when we all get together
     and we know what we're pulling for
and we know who we're pulling against
     then it's time for war
and I pity whatever fool puts himself on the other side
united in mind practice and truth
     we are the overwhelming tide
fit for any and every task
with answers for anyone who may ask
with the evidence of champions complete with the features
we will prevail because we are teachers

Revolting Youth

Once upon a time almost twenty years ago
Five Iron Frenzy recorded a live show
and in 1999 they released the live recording
and the name of the album was perfectly according
Proof That the Youth are Revolting - the perfect title
any visit to a stage for their rock recital
was proof enough for such a description
and soon 1000s caught the subscription
of thinking doing and saying different
captured and promoted everywhere they went
I too saw their show and indeed must say
that its memory is with me to this day
unfortunately the band isn't really around
but their philosophy gained much ground
for the youth of today still maintain
that posture that we adults cannot explain
and may not even like but one thing is true
the youth are revolting if only a few
there is still a remnant seeking the good of others
a revolution for my young sisters and brothers
they haven't given up they're not bolting
they serve as proof that the youth are revolting

For My Son

I walked him on his first day today I walked him on his last
six years of elementary school -
      of course it went way too fast
the clichés and stereotypes get it absolutely right
don't blink because these little ones will soon be out of sight
it still hasn't hit me to be honest - no tears upon my face
the full reality hasn't sunk in
      that he'll never go back to that place
I feel blessed more than anything
      to witness his story unfolding
to see his earliest steps made and know those holding
him accountable to the work at hand
that met him as a boy and
      and stayed with him as a young man
that's where we are now - it's crazy but true
he's done it he's doing it can't wait to see what he'll do
blessed to be a blessing - a bunch times a ton
so glad so humbled so thankful for my son

Good for One More

End of the school year I'm required to reflect
how can I improve? how can I direct
my energy towards higher efficiency?
how can I be a better me?
it's a tall order taken seriously
if I'm not what they need me to be
then so much is at stake so I choose to be aware
and use experience in order to prepare
a better version of myself for the coming year
It'll be a moment before the new kids are here
and I'll start the machine all over again
of turning girls and boys into women and men
it's an honor just to be around such excellent adolescents
I learn just as much being in their presence
don't know how many years I've got in store
but more than thankful that I'm good for one more

Nothing on Monday

Nothing on Monday - what a beautiful thought
better than any present that could ever be bought
summer is here at last - a vacation! bring it on!
everyone has been turned loose -
      the teachers and the students are gone
gone to their well earned rest off to the very best way
captured by three little words - nothing on Monday

Courage and Responsibility
(a tribute to Charlee Skaggs and her family)

There is hope when courage and responsibility meet
and tenacious determination nothing can beat
the potency of such a combination
provides enough power for any situation
any hurdle any discouraging circumstances
any thing where despair possibly advances
cause I know a family where this is the case
courage and responsibility? it's at their place
it's in their hearts lived out in their action
and because of this they are bullseyed by hope's attraction
and what is so remarkable -
      the thing that impresses me the most
is that they consider their efforts
      as never something to boast
their courage and responsibility
      yield humility I cannot measure
and that alone would make this family a treasure
but that doesn't even sum up
      every reason to give them praise
if I were to start a list it would take me days
so know this - they are true and they are right
they are engaged in a struggle
      they are fighting a mighty fight
and its nobility cannot possibly be overstated
it cannot be talked about enough it cannot be overrated
they have no place sitting at the table of despair
discouragement and defeat
this family - this amazing family -
      where courage and responsibility meet

Honor Them

I'm so thankful we have this day of remembrance set apart
to honor those women and men with the bravest heart
who did not consider themselves above others
but gave up their lives for their sisters and brothers
no higher example can ever be given
no greater gift to to all of us living
I remember and I want to do more
for those whose lives were claimed by war
so not only do I remember I also live
I serve I teach I vote and I give
for why did they leave and why did they fight
if not to give us the tools to do what's right?
so I will stand where I am to honor them I'll be true
I will endeavor with courage and bravery
      and honor them as I do

Blessed Structure

I always thought that the free flowing careless mind was the best thing for me
that whatever I felt like doing
      was exactly the best place to be
so glad I know a little better nowadays
happy to subscribe to a collection of better ways
as it turns out I like structure quite a bit
habits and routines? I'll take all of it!
in a place and time when creativity could take a break
what I've got in place provides the stuff to make
content and programming geared to bless the masses
structure for my free flowing mind in absence of teaching classes

A Smile and a Chuckle

How many times in moments boring or sad
tense or upsetting unpleasant or mad
have I said to those who were near
"can you imagine if Joel woulda been here?"
and the response is always the same
a smile and a chuckle imagining he came
because Joel has the gift of erasing frustration
by being able to bring humor to any situation
I know of no one who does it better than he can
count me a supporter indeed a big fan
because he's made me laugh countless times it's true
his timing couldn't be better he's right on cue
so I don't hesitate in this time to stand and proudly say
I thank God for you Joel! Have a happy happy birthday!

A Strong Blessing
(a tribute to Dane McBee and his family)

At the beginning the cloud may seem never declining
a massive source for storms with no silver lining
can it be good? can the night roll into the day?
are there blessings yet to be recognized?
      are we gonna be okay?
I can't say from experience but I can repeat what I've heard
I know a few things and I've got a good word
there's this one story about burdening weight
disadvantages served on one family's plate
it was them it was then but it's different now
their example warrants emulating and how
their solutions flooded their problem's limits
their challenge ultimately failed to prohibit
their success and renewed perception
defense turned offense with jaw dropping interception
running 100 yards straight to the end zone
dancing in victory to reap what was sown
not a one time deal but a cycle repeating
witnessing hope and strength
      while weakness leaves retreating
now they're far from done and their vision may lose its sight
they may stumble a bit lost in the darkness of night
but mostly their days will see great reductions in stressing
for they have found their strength to turn weakness into
blessing

Choose My Family

You can choose your friends but you can't chose your family right?
perhaps that's a worn out phrase that lacks clarity of sight
perhaps you can choose your family and perhaps we should
perhaps that would lead us all to a place of great good
      the thing is today I did
I chose the members of my family I grew up with as a kid
my brothers - I choose them as often as I can
and right now we're on vacation
      so being together is the plan
I'm so glad together we've chosen each other
these great men - much love for my brothers

The Ex-Girlfriend Phenomenon

In relationship politics there is a phenomenon
a practice girlfriends have once that status is gone
whether they're dumped or they do the breaking
their response the next day is very similar in making
if you've ever broken up you know what I'm talking about
she's smoking hot the next day and you just want to pout
it's not fair and you know she went out of her way
just to show you what you're missing just to ruin your day
I call this the ex-girlfriend phenomenon and it happens everywhere
you break up and the very next day there she is right there
wearing your favorite outfit with her hair perfectly in place
smiling right at you a model of confidence and grace
it's kinda funny but as a married man this is still in my life
I've experienced this phenomenon
     as it's been dealt by my wife
now don't worry we're not breaking up or anything like that
we're doing pretty good
     I'm mostly comfortable where we're at
but this weekend I'm out of town
     and I'd like for you all to know
that she has achieved hot mom status
     rocking without me solo
the pictures she's been sending me are arrows to my heart
plenty of proof that she is as beautiful as she is smart
my only consolation indeed my only win
is that I'll be back in just a few days
     and we'll be together again

Honestly Feeling
(a tribute to the Zimmermans)

The temptation to minimize these mountains is very real
facing them honestly seems like too much to feel
and someone else is always facing more so we justify
we turn away a robust defense and exchange it for a comfortable lie
and I get it - oh I get it so much
I get how attractive numbness is
      compared to the reality of touch
when what we feel is the last thing we would ever ask for
when what we feel leaves us raw and broken on the floor
but sometimes we felt what we felt and we were rewarded
and the more this was the case
      the more the truth was reported
we realized that we could be honest
      and not be so self-shielded
and even in that we discovered blessings that were yielded
cause even though we didn't need these hard times
      to love each other well
it was shaped nevertheless and in the end we can tell
that we were surrounded by people on every side
we were never alone so hope never died
and now with a touch more honesty we're ready for more
more mountains and challenges we're ready for war
good thing too because we have an army now
no we're not perfect and we don't always know how
to do exactly what we're supposed to do but hey we do well
so glad to know you know our story so glad we can tell

Home to My Woman

A weekend of catching up with bros -
      oh my word was it fun!
minimal difficulty minimal drama
      maximal enjoyment for everyone
looking forward to doing it again whenever that may be
today though there's another thought that won't let go of me
there's another idea my brain refuses to let go of
I can't get home fast enough to my love
Florida is too deep and Georgia is too tall
hundreds of miles back to Tennessee feels just like a crawl
Atlanta! Chattanooga! out of my way!
I've got to get home to my woman
      and I'm gonna get there today

Dark Alley Defense

You go to basketball practice to learn basketball
    to play basketball on a basketball court
and it's the same across the board
    you can plug in the values for any sport
except for martial arts - that can happen any place
no ball no hoop all you need is space
to move chop punch and kick
with agility and strength and precision on the quick
to perform feats of power dealt to those who offend
for the sake of protecting in order to defend
friends and family and even you
the will to act and knowing what to do
makes goals and touchdowns a silly pursuit
baskets and points dissatisfying fruit
cause what good are they in the perilous valley?
how helpful will they be in a darkened alley?
martial arts on the other hand could be your best friend
the moves the discipline and the knowledge to defend

Wake Your Giants

Wake up your giants there's power to discover
their slumber benefits no one there are blessings to uncover
you have a few walking around
      but how many more could there be?
what breathes in the deepest reaches of your cave
      that you cannot see?
what giants did you once know that have fallen asleep again
wake em up! they're still in there
      their sleeping is not the end
I woke up one of mine today and it really made me wonder
how many more are still in there buried hidden under
there's no telling what I could be making
if I had more giants awaking
let's make some noise at the gate and in the deep
let's get em up and moving don't let your giants sleep

Surrounded by Friends

The bad guys always want to kill the good guys
      but the good guys just wanna be friends
the bad guys tolerance level is zero
      so they wanna bring dissenters to their ends
this can be metaphorical but literal as well
unable to stomach sharing heaven
      they're very confident in who's going to hell
I'm sure the irony has not escaped your understanding
but I do find it helpful in exposing those demanding
measures they cannot possibly meet
the idea of relating to anyone different is an impossible feat
the only thing they can think of doing instead
      is a massive shutdown
not seeking to make peace they only strive to put down
all who they perceive to stand in their way
these are the bad guys and at the end of the day
their thoughts ways and ideals shall not endure
of this you can be sure
the good guys will not have struggled in vain
surrounded by friends they will remain

The Answer is Yes

Can there be sense out of all these mixed up tales?
is there an overriding theme that prevails
above the chaos flowing wild and free?
serving a pattern for you and me?
if so can we know it can we perceive its bend
on our way as we journey on to our end
courage in fear solace in stress?
so glad to say the answer is yes

Emotional Honor

Action wants to happen but it needs provocation
thankfully we all have an embedded invitation
present in our hearts prone to repulsion or attraction
it is our emotions that produce a lot of action
and they are as complicated as the day is long
they are as right as they are wrong
but regardless of their state one thing's for sure
they are inherently valuable so they will endure
though they be abused misused and magnified
malnourished starved and outright denied
they cannot possibly be eliminated
so it's only a matter of when they'll be demonstrated
honor them and they will submit to your lead
dishonor them and they will be your master indeed
it would be wise to treat them with respect
acknowledge their value and wisely direct
secure along the path day to day
let emotions have their say

Something worth Celebrating
(a tribute to Tom and Sandy Koentop)

One confident bachelor with supposedly no plans to attach
encountered destiny and met his match
no hesitation as neither one tarried
six months later the two of them were married
when it's meant to be it's meant to be
no need to hang around to see
if any better offers come along
cause anything else would just be wrong
so the journey began in the right direction
with ecclesiastical support and spiritual connection
they journeyed down the road together
through the good and bad and all kinds of weather
family dynamics on the ground floor
to waiting anxiously while he's off to war
becoming parents both surprised and planned
and both yielding evidence of God's good hand
in seasons of trying struggling and growing
the 70s 80s and 90s they kept on going
in the 2000s 10s and teens they're still here
decades roll on and they persevere
through disappointment and depression stage by stage
and it is love that shows up on every single page
it is love that binds them soul to soul
and they are golden - oh my word -
      not in part but the whole
is something worth observing and emulating
what they have is something worth celebrating

It Takes All Three

You can't win with your mind
you can't win with your heart
you can't win with your strength
it takes all three
a victory in only one of those departments
      is certainly no victory for me
but a victory in all three is truly saving the day
such a victory is permanent and cannot be taken away
so if something is worth seizing give it all ya got
half measures avail nothing they'll just get you caught
but when your mind heart and strength are not divided
and they are instead equally united
doors will swing wide open for you
so many possibilities available to do
not a thing in the world will you lack
so I ask you now "what's holding you back?"

The Editor's Resignation

Growing up I lived everywhere
      it's just how my story played
but I always wonder what it would've been like
      if I woulda stayed
in just one place 'stead of moving every fall
but honestly I can't stand that thought at all
cause there's not one person I want to erase
I don't wanna cross off the address of one place
even in those places where I barely remained
even they lead to something gained
even they had a blessing for my mind
before I moved on and left them behind
who am I anyway to wish for an edit?
He's used all of it so I give him credit
for using these experiences to make me me
so every day and everything
      was just as it was supposed to be

More than Proof

We got married when Bill Clinton was president
    gas was a $1.07
and if you wanted to walk your buddy
    to his flight gate you were able to
a lot has changed in fifteen years
    and even more so for me and you
three states three kids and more growing up
    than I can measure
good times bad times but all of it is a treasure
the pain the trouble the doubt and fear
the struggle the heartache year after year
are reminders right down to the ounce
that what we have is certainly what counts
because you know the price we've paid
just to get this far with what has been made
and I'd do it again in a heartbeat with you
I'd stick it out through and through
these fifteen years are more than proof enough
that God has us even when times are rough
He's the only way we're still making it
even in those times when we were faking it
He knew better and brought us with His Hand
into abundance His promise His truth His land
so glad it's you and I standing right here
so ready to rock it with you one more year

Tenderness all Over the Place

The world is not always as tough as it may seem
we are much closer to being on the same team
and by my reckoning we are winning
and it's not just the way we're story spinning
our observations lead us to something worth knowing
from the morning commute to the light night going
I see tenderness poured out all over the place
a thousand little entry points
      that contribute to the flow the grace
frequently subtle so more often than not
you've got to be watching or you'll be missing a lot
I promise you they're there - they're there every single day
the question is whether we'll see them
      or will we walk on our own way
let's help each other shall we? let's get tenderness in view
I sure could use your assistance
      and I'm more than happy to assist you

Born in the Spring
(for Lee and Melody Bowling)

Spring began and everything was new
they noticed each other and love was in view
a trip across state lines marked their start
and they began their journey to oneness of heart
spring moved into summer and they both could tell
that the strength of their love was was doing well
even in the fall when trouble came
their status continued just the same
but winter was unlike before
struggles came on more and more
leaves withered and fell to the ground
but in the end the tree was still found
holding on to life able to survive
winter passed and the tree was alive
the freezing temperatures couldn't take what they had
spring's good trumped winter's bad
warm on the inside only outside shaking
now spring is here again and we witness the making
of husband and wife - what a beautiful beginning
tested and tried yet shining they're winning
the love that God made is making and will make
the love born in the spring that winter couldn't take

Thankful and Mindful

It's never a problem to lay down
      on a blanket on the ground under a tree
summertime and I'm a teacher -
      every moment feels good to me
no classes no lessons no papers to grade
just me and my family sitting in the shade
with a breeze making the afternoon so nice
sweeter than a mason jar of sweet tea on ice
and I'm thankful and I'm mindful for what's going on
I know all this changes
      and in a moment all this will be gone
so I soak it up every chance I can
so thankful to my Father - I am a blessed man

The Mimosa

The only thing I know about trees is what I'm able to view
I don't know much but I like to watch
     to find out what they do
and I've noticed my mimosa tree every single year
and how late in the spring its blossoms appear
there are trees all over my neck of the woods punctuating
the landscape of all our neighborhoods
and it's so nice when spring comes around
and the trees blossom all over town
but it's strange when I watch the mimosa tree
and why it waits so late is a mystery to me
but then I was encouraged by that one thing
the mimosa isn't competing to bloom first in the spring
it just does what it does slow and steady
and then it blooms when it is ready

Casually Intentional
(a tribute to Darren and Kim Frank)

They were just hanging out it was just conversation
no pressure no plan just old fashioned communication
would yield results neither one could have predicted
but certainly benefitted from the good that went with it
looking back they can see exactly what they were making
a foundation able to withstand the sort of shaking
found in relationships everywhere
their story was better because their care
was casually intentional with good habits every day
and the payoff has been much more than I can say
but I will say I'm inspired observing what I see
the two of them model such humility to me
such grace such patience such attention to relating
to each other not another on each other they're waiting
to proceed she for him and certainly him for her
going to the next thing together will occur
and it is beautiful such an example
they model it well and their blessing is ample
twenty years! it's amazing! so happy they're well!
so thankful they have such a story to tell

Poetry Driven

Poetry is a great driver but when she's alone in the car
most folks don't care where she's going
      even if she's going far
but on the other hand if poetry had a rider
if there is another sitting beside her
it is much more likely folks will want to know
where poetry is going with her friend in tow
and poetry has lots of friends all over the place
she makes friends easily in a wide array of space
like humor grief and narration
worship honor and inspiration
when these friends travel while poetry's at the wheel
it actually becomes a pretty big deal
poetry alone? not many wanna go near it
but when ideas are poetry driven everybody wants to hear it

Love Trouble

I'm not looking for trouble
      but there's a few things I'd welcome it for
I'd take trouble for who and what I love
      for that I'd go to war
and just so we're clear on the matter allow me to say
that I only love a few things and people
      and that's just my way
I don't love politics entertainment or education
sports of any kind or governmental station
I don't love planes trains or any kind of cars
I don't love the sun the moon or even the stars
I love people specifically my family
I'd get into all kinds of trouble for what they mean to me
but more than my parents my kids and my wife
I love my Savior, Jesus Christ - He gave me life
I haven't gotten into any trouble yet
      but I assume that will change
Jesus gives life but some think it strange
or unbelievable or implausible or a straight up lie
Jesus loves everyone why else would He die?
why else would He rise again to proclaim His resurrection
why else would He spend every minute daily
      to get us in the right direction.
I'd gladly get in trouble for Him who I cannot see
I'll gladly take whatever may come
      'cause He took it all for me

Provision for Strength

I have no strength and I know that I don't
I can pretend but I know I won't
be able to stand before opposition
there is no defense in my position
so I trust in a God Who is enough on His own
to provide for me when I'm tempted to go it alone
His provision is very real there's no mystery about it
and today as I was tempted to doubt it
His Grace manifested itself to belief
and in Jesus' Name my soul found relief
when I called out I was able to seek
my brothers were my strength when I was weak

The Key to Joy

The door to joy is locked and few have the key
few understand what is required if its capture is to be
the key to joy is avoided by most though it is very good
the key to joy is sadness though it is oft misunderstood
for it may seem that they exist in oppsition
impossible cooperation irreconcilable position
but they actually have a partnership and a good one too
sadness and joy coming through
bringing you and me through all kinds of stuff
both are required to get over what's rough
Sadness for acceptance and joy for optimism
without both it's just perpetual pessimism
which will cripple malign and destroy
sadness is the key to unlock joy

On Writing

You never know what will happen when you start writing
the endless possibilities are fantastic and exciting
between beginning and end
      there is so much to be gained
so much to be understood and so much to be explained
but by far my favorite above all that I know
is the wonder in where your writing can go
and where it can take you I must say it is worth
mentioning it can take you to the ends of the earth
and beyond - it's true - your words can save
your writing is your memory beyond the grave
you will live on after you're dead
your writing will go on to say what you said
you just never know what can happen when you do
your writing is your voice your writing is you

Blood and Spirit

Where does he get it? Where does his goodness come from?
what contributors comprise the values
      that give my dad his great sum?
I know he got a few things from his dad but that's not all
it was blood and Spirit responding to the call
of raising my father to the man he became
for he himself testifies to each of them by name
he reveres them in memory and honors them in deed
he bears the fruit from their planted seed
and honestly I don't know all of them
I am hard pressed to give a proper account
      of those who influenced him
but I know they were there giving him what he needed
and I couldn't be more thankful
      for what was so deep seeded
integrity commitment humor and passion
and a sense of adventure topped with compassion
so glad the Spirit moved men to lift
the life spirit of my father who is such a gift

Holy Reality

Reality may not be what you suppose
every day life and how it goes
isn't everything it's cracked up to be
there's much more out there for you and me
tonight was an example of all this
and sometimes I'm tempted to miss
the significance found in a public display
acknowledging God all the way
in Spirit and truth He is so near
with 1000s of his children He is here
His Presence in this place is so much
responding to Him and His touch
He is here I raise my hands to declare
I raise my voice aloud in the air
increase Your presence so that I may see
in all times in all places have your way in me

Kingdom Movement

The Movement is permanent it's not going away
it will be here long after today
and tomorrow and the day after that one too
the perfection of the movement insures it is true
despite attempts to the contrary
and some were even terrifyingly scary
the Movement is always bigger than the sum of its parts
always deeper than all our hearts
it's His heart that moves in one accord
regardless of who is on board
but you wanna be on this train trust me
moving unimaginably fast it is free
it's The Movement the Kingdom in short His reign
yielding levels of courage none can explain
why else would we do what we do
if we didn't have eyes with the Kingdom in view
but it's the perspective held by true believers
an outpouring making us crazy receivers
perhaps you've seen the response to such a gift
a turning of saints in an infinite lift
approaching the throne of the King of kings
the Maker Creator and Author of all things
Architect of the Kingdom in which they reside
they are satisfied with where they abide
and the evidence is clear - look at how they respond
in word in truth there is such a bond
that exists among the worshippers on their feet
He is their all in Him they're complete

Assistance

The only way out is hand in hand
strength in numbers is not so much a demand
but a requirement for passage across
otherwise expect to incur great loss
when trying to leave on your own
the truth is no one gets out alone
a buddy a friend a brother if you will
all possible assistants for getting over the hill
better yet a mentor shepherd mom or dad
could be the best you ever had
just get out of there just go while you can
do it - all you need is a hand

You're the One

It's You it's all about You and that is as it should be
I won't try for a moment to make it about me
Your presence Your glory outshine all others
captivated by its wonder with my sisters and brothers
Your children responding to all that You've done
in this world in our lives it is You You're the One
Who does it all no other compares
to You our Redeemer who takes all our cares
all our burdens all our shortcomings and sins
and turns them around to permanent wins
that's what You do that's Who You are
that's why I wanna be near You never far
that's why I'm so glad You are right here
and wherever I go I can go without fear
because You're there You're worthy
      You're holy You're enough
my safety my rock my shelter
      my peace when times are tough
our Shepherd our Friend our Provider
      qualified to take the lead
You are all that matters You are all we need

Attraction Wins

I'm only so distractible
in the end I lean more towards attractable
because it's been a busy week with no spare time
but today is another story in my mind
I wish I could say it was a long time ago
but the longing is recent so I already know
that the cure is specific there's only one thing to do
attraction killed distraction so I'm coming for you
and when I get you the whole world will disappear
nothing to see nothing to hear
just someone to hold someone to adore
the one who holds my heart forevermore

Coming Down the Mountain

A mountain top meeting - amazing things were going on
Moses Elijah Jesus Peter James and John
I can't imagine a more stellar cast
but as it goes with all good moments it was not to last
Moses and Elijah disappeared and the rest came down the mountainside
literally and figuratively as the moment quickly died
Peter James and John carried something unique
a blessing in their hearts that none could ever seek
it was a gift given from the One
their friend and master their guide The Son
what a sight what an opportunity
    what a moment it must've been
up there on that mountain for those seven amazing men
and what a letdown what a disappointment
    what a discouragement it became
coming down the mountain to everyone else
    who was still the same
who hadn't seen what they saw nor hear what they heard
no idea what they experienced and not a single word
could possibly give voice to the party they'd just had
despite such a difference in height though it wasn't all bad
they came to nonsense in the valley
    but they still knew what to do
yeah they came down the mountain
    but Jesus came down the mountain too

The Protagonist

It's so easy to lose the plot before the story's end
I'm not sure the enemy is not sure about the friend
not sure what needs to happen in order to make resolution
not sure who actually knows the correct solution
until the true protagonist shows himself so
and every other character knows which way to go
and their significance from that moment to the last
is based on their adherence to the protagonist's vision cast
heroes are declared and villains are recognized
plans are made and allies are harmonized
I sure do love it when the lines are so clear
I sure do love the protagonist right here

Excellent Excellence
(a tribute to Darrell and Kendra Lassiter)

The very excellence he was practicing was the excellence she was looking for
and even when he showed up with it she still demanded more
because she was worth it and so was he
excellence demands excellence
      and that's what they both would see
an idea was born and it really could not have been better
and in the fullness of time they became more excellent together
so they started this excellent journey sharing one name
and time bore witness to that excellence staying the same
in fact the excellence couldn't be contained just between the two
two daughters two sons that excellence grew and grew
and even then with children of their own
they just couldn't keep the excellence for them alone
it began to flood out into the streets and into other towns
their excellence went viral and knew nor respected no bounds
romantically domestically and vocationally too
their excellence couldn't just pick
      one place to blossom into view
thirty four years of it and hundreds have been blessed
hundreds stand in awe and respect to honor the very best
unassuming understanding undeniably understood
to be pillars of virtue full of Grace
      known all over overflowing with good
let it be written and so let it be said
Holy Father let such excellence in Your world be spread
thank You for such examples of just how good it can be
their excellence is Yours evidence for all to see

The Most Important Person

You are the most important person -
      perhaps you needed to hear that today
maybe you're misled by what others may say
or maybe your perception in the mirror is a bit skewed
maybe it's difficult to keep a healthy attitude
about who you see looking back
overly critical about what you lack
here's the thing though this is not flattery
don't mistake humility for personal battery
you are the most important person -
      that's how you were made
and any attempts to discount or degrade
your permanent status before your Maker
is just a subplot from the Liar and the Faker
it's not true so don't believe it
there's better news if you'll receive it
you're an Image bearer a child of the King
wonderfully made and everything
that doesn't affirm this truth can just disappear
chalk it up to lies and propaganda based on fear
you are the most important person - let all doubt be gone
and when you do do me favor won't you? pass it on

Know Strength

Every white knuckled moment stands to testify
that my strength only serves as an avenue to die
whether it's sooner or whether it's later
temptation's gravity is always greater
when I try to rock it solo and not include my team
the end result is pain and failure no matter what it may seem
in the beginning at the start of a matter
self-reliant confidence will cause my soul to shatter
in a million pieces scattered to the night
with no hope no return no happy ending in sight
does all this make sense? am I being clear?
do you understand how doomed I am
      when I'm the only one here?
as it stands I thank God I'm not
my team serves its purpose well and I am not caught
none of us are - we look after one another
side by side sister to sister brother to brother
it's a beautiful thing it's life it's true
it's the will to risk to love to do
more than we could ever do alone
it's the community of intimacy -
      of knowing and being known
the best team I can imagine fit for every task
established by my Father for better I cannot ask

Definition of Enemy

They're not the enemy - whoever they are
no matter how sharply you disagree no matter how far
your conclusions are from one another may be
no human can ever be your enemy
but you do have an enemy oh yes you do
and he has nothing but hatred and contempt for you
his will for you is despair and isolation
discouragement and ultimately elimination
physical for sure but spiritual as well
his goal is to drag you straight to hell
and if you suppose that any man is your enemy
then he has you exactly where he wants you to be
but if you accept that our struggle is not against man
then count yourself in opposition to the devil's plan
and furthermore if you wanna be a hit
then get down on your knees before God and submit
to His rule His plan His Kingdom His reign
and even when others call you insane
be confident because they're not the enemy anyway
pray for them though and be steadfast in what you say
and how you act and in what you do
let Love be the definition for everything about you
Love is the truth Love is what's real
Love is the maker of the only deal
that will get you through all of this
so please listen closely please don't miss
the Hand that is always reaching out
in the tension between your faith and your doubt
in the whelming flood that monopolizes
so much of our time as it criticizes
both sides but hold on hold on don't fuss
there's no such thing as sides there's only us

Love one another that's what He said from the beginning
do this and even losing we'll be winning
do this and our enemy will be forced to flee
do this and watch them be transformed to we

Truly Alive

Your goodness still impresses even amazes to this day
I can't make this stuff up Your favor Your way
leave me in such a place the last place I deserve
You take steps to show Your love You dress down to serve
while I'm still thinking about me myself and I
Your servant leadership comes down from on high
and You show me what Love is without a bit of shaming
You model it professionally and never resort to blaming
I want to get it I want to be true
I absolutely want to forget about myself
      and lose all of me in You
because You're reality You are what matters
You are the solid Word
      crushing all my self-centered chatters
You are good to a degree I can't compare
You are always available You always care
for us who miss the point much more often than not
the Unchanged Changer who makes the way for those who
would otherwise be caught
erase me and write Yourself in I don't want to survive
only when I'm covered in You will I be truly alive

Among Folks Celebrating

Leaving in the dark returning the same
what a long day! but so glad we came
even if I'm worn out from head to toe
exhaustion is the proof that lets me know
today's value can't be summed up in hours
but something more like candy or flowers
that is to say it was a treat or a gift
with specific properties that served to lift
the spirits of those participating
very common among folks celebrating

Use Freedom Well

It's been a tough year like all the rest
you've seen fire you've been put to the test
I've been ashamed of you and I've been proud
you've done things that I wish were not allowed
but you've also done things that are very fine
despite all your inconsistencies I'm proud to call you mine
and that's a big deal because my loyalty isn't light
but I believe in your ideals and I even believe your might
used in the right way can be and has been good
others have been blessed by you
      in the global neighborhood
and it's not just you - what am I saying? - it's us
it's 239 years of fighting failure and fuss
no small amount of quarreling has gone in our relationship
it is our freedom that causes our successes
      as well as moments to slip
and they are many - far too many to count
but our failures are not our definition
      as we ascend freedom's mount
let's use our freedom well and let this year stand to testify
that Love alone defines us from soil to sky
and let's give each other more reasons to say
let freedom ring for all in this land - God bless the USA

The Point of No Return
(for David and Michelle Nimmo)

All couples face the point of no return
the point where destiny is clear and in a moment you learn
that your life is over and your life has begun
she is his he is hers and soon the two shall be one
some couples arrive early while others arrive late
and sometimes this point can be realized as early as the first date
if you believe in coincidence then this story is a buffet
but if you believe in the Will of the Divine then believe me when I say
that no man could have orchestrated the events that lead up to this
it was God alone who can be credited for such romantic bliss
because it was a date that wasn't a date but really it was
she didn't intend he didn't intend they were kayaking just because
they thought it would be a pleasant occasion
but in fact they both fell to a greater persuasion
two hours became a day and a day became much more
the point of no return they were changed at the core
their minds heard their hearts and there would be no denying
that the love between the two of them existed without even trying
that's what you call effortless such a blessing shared
when his love for her grew so big that it had to be shared
and its return while significant came as no surprise
since it had already bloomed fully in both their eyes
never to fade never to die never to depart
they'd passed the point of no return united in love they share one heart

Fears Celebrations and Emotions

My feelings after living the sixth of July
2015 go from low to high
there was anger sadness and pity it's true
but there was gratitude gladness and celebration too
I know it's not unique to feel both in one day
but today was different in the way
I felt them both to such degrees
from clapping my hands to hitting my knees
in such close proximity to certain things
and what was dealt and how it brings
so much pain to those on both sides
folks with whom my soul abides
and who are caught in such a raging rain
and I want to be the one to take away their pain
but all I can do is sit watch and feel
and that's why the whole thing sucks for real
I want to fix it all and save the day
let Jason be the hero I'll show the way
good grief that sounds dumb I sure have some pride
I'm glad this is the dialogue playing inside
of my head as my thoughts go back and again
what a trip as I reflect on the choices of men
I'd probably do better as I'm sorting what I'm feeling
and let God be the One Who brings all the healing
He knows full stories much more than I
what a Redeemer! so glad I can cry
all my fears celebrations and emotions
to the One who stills storms and lets men walk on oceans

Life is the Worst

Life comes at us hard with fast balls curve balls
        and knuckle balls
bean balls that nail us additionally lousy calls
from umpires on the take owned by the opposition
everything stacked against us might have us wishin'
that we'd never bothered to sign up at all
but it's actually worse because life ain't baseball

Life comes at us with crappy teammates poor coaches
        and fans that don't care
interceptions incomplete passes
        and linebackers that won't dare
protect you from getting sacked by the scariest of foes
life is hard! y'all know this is how it goes
you get tossed all over the field fall after fall
but it's actually worse than that because life ain't football

Life is dirty there are no rules
rednecks thugs gangsters and fools
just trying to make it through the night
desperate enough to go ahead and unite
because going solo is certain suicide
foolhardy confidence before a sky scraping tide
will get you nowhere you want to be
there are no heroes take it from me
unite with some dudes that have your back
boots bottles and brass they'll use to attack
find someone you can trust find a team and you'll survive
take every measure you can and you just might stay alive
the morning will come when you make it through the night
        life is the worst life is a fight

Kindness is Welcome

I can't think of an occasion or situation
where kindness is not met with the utmost appreciation
in terms of moments where everything is tense
and impatience is heavy on both sides of the fence
or in moments when everyone is nice
the room is laid back and cool as ice
kindness is welcome in every imaginable place
among every group it puts a smile on every face
it's simple - I know - but it bears worth repeating
kindness is welcome here
      it's so much of what we're needing
so much of what is wanted every day month and year
spread a bit around - kindness is welcome here

Verses Versus

The arrangement of these words is a balancing act
the rhythm of the syllables is set up to attract
readers and listeners looking for such fare
that isn't found just anywhere
but here in these lines and in these verses
order attempts to bless amid the curses
that life throws out on a regular basis
with its off beat rhythms in so many places
it confuses takes crushes and kills
but this is peace it invites it stills
the uncertainty created by things that don't make sense
to replace them with things in this present tense
that are gifts to be treasured for all time
against chaos and void here's order with rhyme

True Acceptance

Immaturity leads us to ascribe value to a certain thing
exclusively supporting it
      because we believe what it can bring
is the most important thing that gets us through
when in fact its counterparts are just as important too
and we lose in the end when we elevate
the one thing I hope that it's not too late
to realize the value of it all
may our eyes realize the valuable call
sent out from all the advantages life gives
even if it's painful to the comfort that lives
may we accept it in its appropriate due
may we accept it because it is true

Commitment Tricks

I commit and then I almost always wanna wimp out
why is that? is it fear is is doubt?
that makes me want to go and fold
before I even have a chance to behold
the thing for which I'm committed in the first place
the thing for which I run the race
whether it's big or whether it's small
doesn't actually matter at all
in terms of maintaining my integrity
so my words and actions will always be
one and the same with no quitting
but letting my yes be my yes and not just my spitting
I know it's actually what I want anyway
so when I psych myself out before before the day
I remind myself all in my head
to let my actions follow exactly what I've said

The Heart of Heroism
(a tribute to Chuck Swann)

The heart of heroism is filled with servanthood
the guy who places others first is the greatest agent for good
that is where his strength is found that is how he moves
his humble posture is recognized every time he proves
how much he loves people by meeting their needs
from the least to the greatest he consistently doles out deeds
that give the world hope in collective realization
that heroes still exist right here in our nation
I don't know how else I can describe such humility
let us aspire to such levels of honor indeed may we all be
as selfless as him putting others first
doing what is needed in a moment's burst
whether it's hand holding while exhaling final breath
or storming the gates courageously rescuing from death
or reminding someone all on our own
that even in desperate shame they are never alone
let us be like that let us be like him
not a phase not a fad nor a passing whim
but a permanent fixture on the landscape of the city
whether times are ugly or whether times are pretty
make us servants bound by He Who is the Light
forsaking ourselves loving others ever
        endeavoring to do what's right

Ultimately for Life

Is it good versus bad? truth versus lies?
right versus wrong? foolish versus wise?
to a certain extent it is but far greater it is not
ultimately it is Life versus Death
      but that's not always what we're taught
we're taught that some things are really really bad
and if we do them then God will be mad
but from the beginning that's not what God said
for His prohibitions protected man from being dead
but we chose death so God chose it too
sacrificing Himself was what He chose to do
and three days later He reversed death
resurrection brought Life so we all could have breath
it is good it is true it is right for Him to give
but ultimately He did it so you and I can live

Captured

The camera that captured her image is like she who
captured my heart
I am bound by her pure beauty as I have been from the start
she is so precious she brings happiness to every setting
my precious daughter my little girl
      I won't ever be forgetting
how lofty my opinion of her is she is my morning star
I love her now I love her here
      I'll love her as she even goes far
I don't deserve to be her dad
      she deserves much more than I can be
so humbled by this extraordinary young lady
      easily she's the world to me

Good Investment

A unique chain of events put us together today
we weren't even supposed to be together
    but I think it's better this way
wearing complimentary t shirts running errands
    and taking time to rest
any time invested with my little partner is not only good
    it's the best
there's a lot of other folks I could be helping
    there's an awful lot that could be done
but from his end he's completely relaxed
    because I'm the only one
who is what I am never taken for granted
I'm his daddy and days like this
    are strong foundations planted
just the the two of us united for good blessed to be together
me and my little boy - love him so much -
    truly ain't nothing better

Head Turning Impression

He grew up in a day and it's not like I wasn't looking
I was standing in front of the stove
      to keep an eye on my cooking
but in an instant I turned my head
      and I guess that wasn't the plan
and the next thing I knew was that boy
      had become a young man
and to be honest I like him I like him a lot
his sense of humor his company are worth being caught
I'm impressed with how much I am impressed
my impression is is that he is the best
sign me up to be his fan club's president
and I'll toot his horn one hundred percent
it's a good feeling to watch him grow up before my eyes
but it's great that he is so committed
      as one of the good guys
loving others following closely the example of the One
just can't say enough about my terrific son

Team Dad

It takes more than what I have more than what I can get
if my boy is gonna be a proper man then you can surely bet
that it's gotta be a team effort or failure is on the way
if all I can do for him is wrapped up in me
      then I should just shut it down today
and give up but I know something
      I know something much better
I never intended to do this alone
     so in this area I'm a go getter
I've got team Dad on my side
men in his life with whom he can ride
across the wide open range of growing up
and I am not the only man showing up
making a difference speaking truth into his soul
reminding him who he belongs to and who is in control
it means the world that he has other men
      who mentor him as well
he's already reaped the benefit and I for one can tell
that when his days go dark and everything is bad
he will be well supported by the members of Team Dad

Plugging and Pouring

This is how we look and where we are today
it is only for a moment and then it will go away
to be replaced by how we look and feel in the next chapter
but going back is not an option there is only ever after
so for now I am soaking it up indefinitely
these four I'm with - my precious family
are the most important people to me in all creation
my wife and children fill my heart with elation
to such a degree that every fiber of my being
wants to bless every day that we're seeing
seeing together and letting that state be a gift
with the features that inspire and uplift
above the stress and despair in this world all around
pouring myself I am joyfully bound
to these folks who make every day a joy to start
I plug in I pour in because they are my heart

In Good Hands

Sometimes I need to remind myself of what I already know
the Hands that have me are Good
      and come what may even as I go
down roads and up hills that that were never on my list
I'm in Good Hands in every turn and twist
I may not be okay I may not be satisfied
but I will be frustrated tested and tried
I will be broken down and at times wracked with doubt
but if I'm in Good Hands it will all eventually work out
if not now then definitely later
by the One Who exceeds all ideas of Greater
and you know it may not work out while I'm alive
the whole thing may crash down while few if any survive
but I'm still in Good Hands whether or not I have breath
I'm in Good Hands even after death

Unforgettable View

I took some mental pictures today
      that I want to lock in my brain
images to easily access and recall
      on a trip down memory lane
since I didn't have the tech necessary
      to photograph in the ocean
and there were significant memories made
      packed with strong emotion
you see a bunch of us were having fun out there in the water
extended family my wife my big boy and my daughter
but my little boy - my two year old - just didn't wanna get in
he couldn't shake his fear of the water
      and relax to take a swim
but today he did! today he let go of his fear
in his mother's arms he found his happy place -
      what a joy to be so near
what a joy indeed as I got to hold him too
my little fella splashing with mommy and daddy -
      what an absolutely unforgettable view!

Candles in a Pinch

Man's inventions are likely to fail if not sooner then later
we live our lives conveniently
        and our tech really knows how to cater
to our every whim and desire and it's nice for a while
but in a pinch it's good to have something
        that can go the extra mile
because eventually all our gadgets will fail
        eventually they will die
when that happens I find it best
        to have some candles nearby

Team Family

Fewer things are more complicated than family
rarely do things go as we want
      I know that's how it goes with me
and my own and extended family as well
people living together - boy there's some stories I could tell
but the point is there's gonna be sunshine
and there's gonna be rain
there's gonna be easy and there's gonna be pain
there's gonna be conflict and loads of frustration
but there never has to be any isolation
the thing about family whether big or small
is that when one of you has your back against the wall
when one of you is sick and not getting better
you get down to it and pull together
no matter how bad anything may seem
you stick up for your family
      because your family is your team

Big Catch

I rise and shine earlier than I usually do
to add another experience that's new
with my father-in-law my brother-in-law and my son
and the moment my line is cast I've already won
because I've been fishing before but never like this
never with so much I never wanna miss
like the value of these men and this young man
If fellowshipping with them were the only plan
then that would be sufficient but I get even more
waves crashing knee high rolling in on the shore
with the Atlantic sunrise lighting the way
what a picture at the start of my day
and for a moment I'm alone standing there in the ocean
my heart and mind are captivated by the notion
that this morning is exactly what it is supposed to be
we didn't catch a thing and that is alright with me
we're not walking to the beach house with any fish to fry
we got something better and the simple reason why
is we surrendered the outcome to gain something better
the serene scenery and most of all being together

Seas and Skies

Landlocked we can only see so much with our eyes
but our whole planet is dominated by seas and skies
how easy it is to get caught up on land
and forget the bigger picture that is much more grand
with North America behind and the Atlantic in full view
my eyes bless my mind with the morning sky hue
how easily I forget that Earth is much more than I see
if God can handle that then I reckon He's got me

Love You Anyway

Everybody needs "I love you anyway"
with unkind moments and all the wrong things to say
we need that commitment from our friends and family
for who among us is always what they're supposed to be
try as I might I gotta confess
that I'm not fun to be around when I'm a mess
as a husband and certainly as a dad
there are hours and even days when I am just bad
so I need that "love you anyway" love as much as any
as my character flaws add up to be many
never earned only given as it is completely free
I have this love for my family so glad they have it for me

Making a Difference
(a tribute to Monica Darbyshire)

Hero work is rarely portrayed on comic book pages
on little screens big screens or video game stages
but out on city streets taking calls every night
facing death fully and putting up a fight
on behalf of those in the most desperate situations
where tragedy has interrupted their immediate destinations
but Destiny makes a move to intervene
and there she is right at the scene
the injured couldn't ask for a better one
than my friend who will pull every stop to get it done
two books two rules and one philosophy
if I was hurt I can't imagine anyone I'd rather see
than this awesome sister with a golden soul
making a difference is her goal
so if a life can be saved then she absolutely will
use her knowledge strength experience and skill
to get that person to a place of rest
for healing and wholeness saved by the best
but if a life is finished and the end draws nigh
she will guide that soul to the edge of goodbye
giving them exactly what they need
dignity honor a life saver indeed
I thank God for her and her example worth emulating
I thank Him for such an amazing person -
    one we all could be imitating

Painful Evidence

As a matter of fact it is true
and a decision must be made on what to do
because the evidence all points in the same direction
leaving no room for prideful protection
so either deny that a problem is there
and disregard everyone that could care
or get over it and do what needs done
it's going to hurt and it won't be fun
the evidence is evident - no further need to be weighed
and answers will be presented
      through the choices that are made

One of Us

Summertime in Tennessee is a lot of wonderful things
especially for us for all the good time it brings
three kids whose parents are both teachers as well
and a whole summer together so I can honestly tell
that as sure as we get sick of each other
        we love each other too
and while we're doing all that loving we've got plenty to do
like investing time with extended family
        specifically my niece
all three of our kids love her to pieces
        so the good times never cease
the daughter of my oldest brother
        I'm proud to call her family
her cousins feel even more so and they're always asking me
if she's gonna be any place we go
and if she's not then their answer is no
but if she is then regardless of the weather
they're happy as can be just being together
we sure do love her hanging out is a must
so glad that she is one of us

All the Way Good

Moderate morality makes memories minuscule
it's completely forgettable if it's neither hot nor cool
neither committing to be the hero nor the villain
content to be a bystander on the sidelines chillin
be good be bad but don't be in between
be memorable and be willing to make a scene
not for your name nor for your glory
but rather so there's no doubt who you are in the story
while I'm at it I will strongly suggest you choose to be good
not because it's fun nor easy nor because I think you should
but because the world needs more heroes -
    people doing what's right
people not looking to their own interests
    but being willing to fight
willing to stand outside the boundaries of moderation
engaging the culture in reality with no hesitation
jumping on opportunities while others stop and stare
inspiring those waiting for examples to do and dare
beware the bad guys because your good will push their bad
their reaction to your righteousness
    will by no means make them glad
but don't let it stop you -
    your stand was bound to cause waves
just keep being all the way good
    for consistency is what paves
the road to improvement with gains slower than slow
keep putting in work when days are high and low
it's worth it all though everything may be the cost
when all is given for good nothing that matters is lost

Not the Poem I Wanted to Write

My feelings capture my creativity
    and my heart is anything but light
and the poem in my mind is not the one I wanted to write
but what can I say when my heart is sad
and people disagree because they feel so bad?
it just seems wrong superficial and fake
if I sought to manipulate and make
up words that I don't feel
even when I'm sad I wanna keep it real
the authenticity is so important even though unpleasant
feeling my feelings has value simply being present

There's Always Something

There's always something to write about
there's always something going on
you can say there's not but I have no doubt
that ideas and opportunities won't soon be gone
and by opportunities I'm stretching the boundaries
of what your imagination will permit
because these games have liberal referees
free your expectations go ahead and forget
the rules you have on what inspires
it's much more than you think
simple things can light your fires
and get you way past the brink
of tradition and boring interpretation
there's only one thing you have to do
if you're engaged in regular respiration
then that is all that's required of you
yes - just breathe - nothing more
that would be amazing conceptually
the actions taking place present at the core
are evidence you're made beautifully
and beautiful ones make beautiful things
no flattery here nor attempt to mislead
you - just you - just what your story brings
is perfect for this world for you are what we need

Defeated by Communities

Bullies are not defeated by heroes
      bullies are defeated by communities
when social constructs leave no room for villains
      the power is robbed from the enemies
heroes can inspire they can even lead the way
but it's the community that has to work -
      united they'll save the day
bullies will be absorbed into the healthy fold
letting go of the fear letting go of the old
choosing love instead choosing what's new
letting fellowship crush isolation
      the positive many convert the negative few

The Greater Good

There is always a greater good in all situations
there are so many possibilities at a variety of stations
that can be explored experienced and engaged
there are endless outcomes to be uncaged
limits were made to be broken and destroyed
the status quo is not for the employed
of He who consistently makes all things new
coincidence? not likely. not probable with His cue
He doesn't waste one pain or pleasure
whether or not they were His measure
He uses both for His purpose to get through
what have you got? what will you do?

Yes No

You can't say yes if you don't say no
choosing the one makes the others go
I think I like yes but maybe I don't
cause when it's time to say no a lot of times I won't
so if I don't say no do I really like yes?
thinking about it gives me stress
because I want to be a yes man for the things that matter
I want to be a no man for the stuff that wants to shatter
my soul because if I am loose with my yes
then very soon they will all be worthless

Heart Love Life

This world just wants to break my heart
shake my heart
corrupt confuse and fake my heart

But You're the One who can make my heart
wake my heart
I trust You with it here take my heart

This world just wants to steal my love
conceal my love
destroy bury and seal my love

But you're the One who can heal my love
feel my love
raise up restore and make real my love

This world just wants to play my life
take away my life
dumb down confuse and delay my life

But you're the One who can say my life
display my life
so gladly before You I lay my life

Wrong or Thirsty?

A moment is all we have this life is over quick
discretion is imperative when we get ready to pick
the content of our words and actions
do we choose prohibitions or instead offer attractions?
suppose someone is about to drink poison
      and you realize what they're doing
instinctively you want them to stop
      the course of action they're pursuing
you could yell make a scene
      and knock the cup out of their hands
vindicated by your right standing
      however coercive your demands
or you could offer them water to drink instead
letting the goodness flow within
      forsaking decisions based on dread
the truth is so many want the poison inside
millions seek it but not one is satisfied
in the moments that we have let's turn on the light
and focus less on what's wrong and more on what's right
the poison will be revealed in time of course it's gonna stink
but if we don't share a cup of water they'll never get a drink

Unstoppable Force

A little bit every day beats one day of a lot
steady as it goes and you'll seldom get caught
the blessed hassle of good habits sure is hard to start
but once it gets going it'll be your beating heart
like a two ton train coming down the track
it'll knock over anything that's foolish enough to attack
what's that word that speaks about power on the run?
ah! momentum that's it I can't think of any better one
turn it up slow and stay on course
keep it up daily and you'll be an unstoppable force

A Common Gift

X-Men Harry Potter and Percy Jackson as well
couldn't be more profound in the lengths they go to tell
the sort of stories that are as meaningful as fun
you have unique powers but you're not the only one
everybody needs to hear stories like that
and everyone needs to fellowship
      with like minds where they're at
it's beautiful to get others while they simultaneously get you
encouragement flows and all involved become more true
to the person who they were made to be
more than ears hear and more than eyes see
rather hearts touch and spirits likewise lift
great satisfaction is gained by the sharing of a common gift

Truth That Saves Lives
(a tribute to Clark Flatt
and The Jason Foundation)

Friends reveal themselves
      when they push us to do the impossible
when they stretch with us to find logic in the illogical
empowered we then become defenders for the defenseless
and we are able to make sense
      of what otherwise seems senseless
our eyes are opened to truths once unseen
we see the signs with senses sharp and keen
where once we would have had fear and reasons to doubt it
we now have courage and knowledge
      in order to do something about it
his friends did this for him now he does it for all
tirelessly working toward the goal following the call
he diversifies his methods to get the message out
many avenues are included for all contain a possible route
from football coaches to legislators
and country artists to educators
so many are interested in helping him succeed
because it is not just him but everyone indeed
who benefits from the truth he is constantly speaking
the truth that the needy need us all to be seeking
the truth! oh how I pray that it always survives
this truth in our minds is truth that saves lives

Chain of Encouragement

Don't underestimate your ability to make someone's day
false humility may ensnare and you may wanna downplay
the significance of your words and actions
    spoken to a friend
or a co-worker or an employer
    but let me tell you once you send
those positive words out there into space
you never know just how long
    your encouragement will grace
the listener who needed to hear just what you said
your words lift their spirits now
    they walk with upturned head
now they'll pass it on to someone who needed it too
and so on and so on and to think it all started with you

The Hardest Thing to Say

One of the hardest things to say is a real downer
a sail wind stealer a confidence drowner
in terms of pride it's the absolute worst
and self-sufficiency blows up in a burst
we'd rather do poorly 'til the last possible end
than admit we can't do it and get help from a friend

Forsake the Labels

Sometimes cowards are brave
they forget their fear rescue and save
sometimes the ugly are beautiful to behold
they forget their imperfections and step forward as gold
sometimes the mean are kind
they forget their impatience relax and unwind
sometimes the selfish serve
they forget themselves and others they observe
and sometimes an idiot has a useful thought
he forgets his stupidity and good ideas are wrought
may we all do what we didn't think we could
may we all forsake the labels that keep us from doing good

Good Times are on the Way

If I had to make a prediction I would have to say
that despite what you've heard good times are on the way
I know you may not want to believe
I realize I may appear naïve
but I prefer to be thought of as enlightened
in a world that constantly wants me to feel frightened
I don't know what's next but I do know how it ends
at the finish line in glory with family and friends
even until then I'm convinced
      there's more to look forward to
if my optimism seems shallow
      then let me gently reassure you
that it is not - there's a rock to which I am tethered
and in that reality I can stand even while weathered
outwardly I am wasting away but inwardly I am renewed
knowing this is life and strength and positive attitude
knowing this empowers me to say
that I believe good times are on the way

Something Better

Do you ever think you know what you want?
so you get out there go on and hunt
for the thing that you believe should belong to you
but then it never comes to view
something else comes along that's better
not exactly letter for letter
yeah it's different but you just didn't know
that this was how good things could go
you go on in victory to do what you do
how do I know? it happened to me too

Help Out

If you want to help and assistance is your mission
then pay attention closely to the following preposition
the word that comes after help most frequently
has a lot to teach you and definitely me
we don't help in across through or under
we help out - and isn't it a wonder
that helping out gets us out of so many things
there is a remarkable freedom
      that helping out certainly brings
out of selfishness out of my head out of pride
out of myself and out of the side
of myself that needs to be left no doubt
what a beautiful thing - so much is gained by helping out

Week Won

I know I need Him now I know I need Him on Sunday
surrounded by my brothers and sisters
    in such a peaceful way
this body of believers is where I belong
united in heart united in fellowship united in song
I want to remember that the Spirit
    isn't limited to these walls and pews
nor is He limited to these few hours -
    oh no - I think He can use
so much more in fact I'd like to seek
His presence His peaceful presence for the rest of the week
I see Him flooding Monday Tuesday and Wednesday
He's already there putting it in order so I pray
for Thursday Friday and Saturday too
His presence is enough He makes all things new
He has what it takes He's got the power to bring
this week is won before it starts
    I'm not worried about a thing

The Learning Teacher

The irony isn't lost from where I'm standing
remarkable to say the least these lessons so demanding
and how what I'm teaching right now seems to be
the very thing that is right on top of me
is there a coincidence to this lesson?
I doubt it - I'd have to say if I was guessin
that encouragement can follow - that's what I'd like to get
the good news is God's not through with me yet

The Distracted Fan

I always forget to watch the game
      whenever I go to the football field
I try to be a supportive fan for my team
      as they attempt to yield
a victory for the night's contest
but alas! my concentration just isn't the best
there's really not much football in my head
so I end up catching up and talking instead
I actually love football games for this very reason
the fall is such a lovely season
outside any night of the week or weekend
is a great investment a great way to spend
time with such interesting women and men
so for that reason I say Go Fight Win!

Shame has Nothing

Shame has nothing for me
nothing
I don't need it and I don't want it
mistakes will be made and that is what that is
but shame wants me to think that I am so bad that no one
could ever understand
that my faults are too great
too unique
too anything
NO!
the truth is not found in thinking like that
behaving like that
or even for a moment wishing that
I would've could've or should've
what's done is done
I gotta move forward
here now I declare
that shame will not ever get me there

Coffee! (the best drink ever)

At some point my taste buds had a change of mind
for most of my life they had been blind
it's hard to imagine I would ever think
that I was less than enthusiastic for the world's best drink
coffee - so smooth and undeniably rich
the world has made its choice and it will never switch
from the cross cultural beverage preferred far and wide
exported everywhere so many countries' pride
I raise my cup with this caffeinated endeavor
here's to coffee! the best drink ever!

The Confident Hand

You can win if you can recognize what you've got
knowing the difference between a little
    and being able to see a lot
separates the losers from the winners
those that leave with loot to snack
    and those that leave with dinners
in a manner of speaking I've got an unbeatable hand
I can go all in with full confidence
    taking my strongest stand
oh I want to recognize that what I've got is the best
I want to recognize the hand I've got
    is sufficient for every test

So Surrounded

Hemmed in on every side it's as beautiful as it is secure
the comfort found in a group of friends
     is therapeutic and pure
to the extent that other comparisons
     are drawn straight from this source
this well this abundance this is the course
that will lead to strength serenity
     comfort and understanding
sealed in love with an unshakable branding
I don't want to imagine how my life would be without it
I know how imperative it is and that's why I'm all about it
an immeasurable blessing Divinely founded
I sigh in satisfaction to be so surrounded

Luckier than the Birthday Girl

Everybody's glad when a pretty girl has a birthday
they bring presents to her party
      and have lots of sweet things to say
she lights up like a candle in response to being celebrated
her grace matches her beauty
      so the praise of her friends is justly stated
the world is balanced the good guys are winning
and everyone is laughing smiling and grinning
in fact there is one man who is smiling more than her
it is not vanity that such joy should occur
but reality and a realization of how blessed he has become
he gets it and he knows where he is from
the pretty girl doesn't leave her birthday party alone
the only one luckier than her is the man that takes her home

Enthusiasm Wonder and Delight

Thank you for the enthusiasm wonder and delight
when you bring such energy you put in me the fight
that isn't willing to settle for less
or even interested in wallowing in the mess
that circumstances and disappointments
      would lead me to do
you inspire me to bring something new
something that's never been done before
something that no one could possibly ignore
grabbing the whole world's amazement and attention
unable to turn away always making mention
of the plus that you are the bonus you've brought
the optimistic energy that the whole world caught

Know This

There's so much I don't know but I do know this
regardless of how often I fail no matter how much I miss
I am loved by my Father the maker of Heaven and Earth
the Love He has for me defines all my worth

Lock and Key

The locks on the mysteries have been changed
what we knew once has been rearranged
and how we used to apply knowledge can no longer be
old solutions won't work we need a new key
and the key that fits the door today
      may or may not work tomorrow
if it won't turn like it does right now
      you may want to go and borrow
someone else's if they're on the edge
      it's best to stay connected
no one can possibly have all the keys
      so in teamwork success is directed
trial and error again and again is the best way to learn
not sure how to unlock the door?
      it'll only open if you give it a turn

People are Worse God is Better

People are worse than you think
there is no limit to how low they'll sink
the so-called good are as bad the bad
the whole of our righteousness is sadder than sad
to hope in even one is an exercise in insanity
to trust in yourself is shallow vanity
I speak as one that knows for I am corrupt too
depraved in thought wicked in what I do
but God is better than you could ever imagine
unlimited and boundless awesome in form and fashion
His love is enough to cover all who live
His Grace is sufficient to abundantly forgive
the wickedness that men do think and are
drawing near His heart even the farthest of the far
His righteousness His power
     is perfection bright and blazing
doing the impossible only ever always amazing
I'm only aware of a fraction of a fraction
infinite and holy beautiful in thought and action

Disappointments

Where do I put my disappointments that happen every day?
how shall I handle all these let-downs
      that constantly come my way?
shall I keep them until they are filled
or ignore them until they are dormant and stilled?
is it best to starve them when they call
and let them leave by doing nothing at all?
these disappointments aren't going away
      they'll be here until the end
experience has taught me
      it's best to share them with a friend

It Feels Good to Say

It feels good to have ideas in my head
to have the drive when I get out of bed
to go and create invent and make
a gift to the world for everyone to take
it feels good to have support for my craft
friends and professionals who I can ask
if what I'm doing is flying or failing
if it is sinking or if it is wailing
it feels good to figure stuff out
to unlock solve and destroy the doubt
that I wouldn't or that I shouldn't
and definitely that I couldn't
I can! it's like that everyday
it feels good to have something to say

Run with the Fliers

If you can stand then stand with the walkers
soon enough you'll be walking too
if you can walk then walk with the runners
soon enough you'll be running too
if you can run then run with the fliers
soon enough you'll be flying too

If you surround yourself with folks as good as you are
then improvement will elude you and you will not get far
but if you seek fellowship with those who are in the lead
then your strengths will multiply and you will surely
succeed

Whispers of Beauty

Hatred fear intolerance and pride
the consumption of the ages on every side
these cannot be outgunned - against them none can win
healing change must come and take place from within
fighting fire with fire is a futile exercise
it is not in shouting that one is counted among the wise
but in the whispers of beauty so rarely used
in the notes of grace to those short fused
the words of life that reverse death
these go within create and sustain love's breath

Weeding Time

I think it's time to weed the garden it's gotten out of hand
it ain't the rain it ain't the climate the season or the land
it's these weeds that are trying to choke
        every good thing I've got growing
I'm tossing seed after seed and I'm continually sowing
but little to no progress is made 'cause these weeds get in the way
I reckon it's time to do some weeding I reckon it's time today

Enough

Your love seeps in through my pours I drink it in and
breathe it as well
I clothe myself with it too
       in order to have the courage to tell
about everything that You have done
You fill me You cover me You're the One
Who provides me with all that I need
You are my God my Father You are all I'll ever need
all I could ever want You always remain
my rock my world my clarity when pain
gets to be too much gets to be too rough
You are my world and You are enough

Walk it Out

Plans fail communication cuts out
      and expectations are not met
when this is the state of things it could surely lead to regret
impatience could rear its ugly head
      and open the door to disconnection
but before that happens there could be a better direction
walk it out - a physical solution yeah I know
but sometimes relationship gridlock
      leaves us no other place to go
whipping the dead horse of wrong and right
sure is a good way to have a bad night
but if you take a walk with your opponent you may see
that whatever it is that is between you
      isn't what you're making it to be
I bet if you walk there will be a happy end
and you will forget your offense and remember your friend

Receive Work Suffer

If you receive it that's a pretty good deal
it is a gift and the favor that you feel
is satisfying worthwhile and true
someone likes and appreciates you
the memory though will eventually fade
even if the impression that was made
was significant you can still bet
that if it was given you may well forget

If you work for it that's a better deal
your wages were earned so now you can feel
justified compensated paid and true
no one else did it - it was just you
the memory though may eventually fade
even if what you earned was made
by really hard work you can still bet
that if you worked for it you may forget

If you suffer for it that's the best deal
the pain the heartache and everything that you feel
puts a mark on your soul that is tried and true
and what you have cannot be taken from you
the fastened memories will never fade
the sorrow borne will surely be made
into a foundation beyond any bet
you suffered for it - you won't forget

Celebrating Momma

One look at the stats page for my site
reveals a truth that yields great delight
concerning someone who always pays attention
it's no surprise that I easily mention
my mother as she is a pretty big fan when I rhyme
I started these verses a while ago
      and she's been around the whole time
the stats don't lie but the story they tell is far from done
there's really no way to quantify a mother's love for her son
nor is there any way to do it the other way around
but attempting to love my momma
      is where I wanna be found
a model for patience wisdom and generosity
loving daddy loving us where she is is a great place to be
a sense of humor easy to talk to such a blessing to us all
today is her day - let's celebrate her y'all!

Little Girl's Birthday

When a little girl has a birthday it's an all day thing
from sun up to sun down her whole world unites to sing
the biggest round of Happy Birthday that has ever been
every corner she inhabits all the women and all the men
rise to wish her the the most glorious year
and how glad they are how proud they are
    that God saw fit to put her here
in this world at this time with this family in this place
and there is no small amount of satisfaction as we see the
response on her face
to celebrate a little girl on her birthday -
    oh my word what an occasion!
even the lowliest pessimistic individuals are raised by the
potent optimistic persuasion
so that everyone around this precious little girl
rejoices that such a soul walks among us in the world
and everything's gonna be alright
    everything's gonna be okay
all because this precious little girl just went
    and had herself another birthday

Dear Lois

Dear Lois,
I can only imagine what it's like every time he leaves
every time he flies away for a world that still believes
that they need him but so do you
and so many hours pass while he is not in view
the life that those who love heroes live
      is every bit just as brave
the sacrifices you make while the one you love goes to save
is just as super if not even more so
silently in the background you remain while he is on the go
and every time he's out doing good you have no guarantee
that he will be back alive and well and feel pleasantly
another hero would rise should he fall from the sky
but are there any equal to him for you?
      who on earth could try?
he is honored on a regular basis
      for his strength and integrity true
I'm writing at this moment in order to honor you
your support and your sacrifice
      are as legendary as his might
the world is only as safe as it is
      because you support his fight
so I thank you for being part of the plan
thank you, Lois, for loving Superman

Be Still My Heart

Be still my heart you have all that you need
let your beat be steady let peace take the lead
through valleys of fear shame and condemnation
avenues of complacency ingratitude and frustration
let none of it quicken your beating
recognize it for the moment that it is fleeting
because it is nothing more than a fickle breeze
a temporary phenomenon not worth your ease
not worth any part of your strength or your will
you have all you need - my heart - be still

For the Love of Books

Books look good on a shelf
but if you don't read you're only cheating yourself
uncracked spines won't enlighten your mind
and dusty edges will only leave you behind
it would be a little better to read
turn some pages underline some phrases
      go and get what you need
knowledge experience and wisdom can be found
in the text filled pages professionally bound
best of all what I would recommend
is practicing what you read with a neighbor or friend
books are good for entertainment's attraction
they're also great as starting points for action
the seeds of revolution may be planted in such pages
and you may hold the script to perform on the stages
but you'll never know relying on yourself
reach on over and take a book off the shelf!

Ignorance the Opportunity

You don't have to know it all nor master every task
you just have to be careful
      that there's always someone to ask
not knowing is not a problem
      since there's probably someone that does
ignorance is an opportunity and the reason is because
not knowing is a wonderful avenue
that takes you to a place where you get out of you
nobody has it all together nobody has every plan
that's why it's such a good deal that I can't but we can

Love Truth Cookies & Wings

Since nothing gold can stay what are we waiting for?
if all the best is on the way out
      and we're not getting any more
then let's soak it up as much as we can
I'd say hugs and kisses are a pretty good plan
for friends and family sure and since this is all about to end
why not take the time and turn an enemy into a friend?
human beings are all made in the Image Divine
it's not like there's just yours and mine
we are all His from the greatest to the least
thinking in those terms will open doors for peace
and love and truth and cookies and wings
if we knew how beautiful we are
      we could share all sorts of things
we were made for fellowship and harmony
not dissension not division
      you're my brother not my enemy
let's lay down our essays of fear
      and pick up our Father's gracious song
and let's get out and do it now
      because we honestly don't have long

Happiness Around Every Corner

There is happiness around every corner -
    at least there is for me
I'm not saying I don't have bad days
    but as you can clearly see
I've got some clear advantages
    when it comes to my perspective
that give me plenty of fuel to maintain
    my optimistic directive
I'm down sometimes it's true
    especially when I make mistakes
but not one to wallow in miserable failure
    I get up because I've got what it takes
I didn't earn it it was a gift
and my response is a life long lift
back up to the One who first gave it to me
like I said around every corner I see
happiness - I've been seeing it for a while
I have more reasons than ever to keep walking with a smile

Her Brother

He hurt her
he hurt her deeply consistently and without measure
she was a queen a star an absolute treasure
but he didn't recognize her in any of these ways
and so it went at the end of their days
the one intended for her protection
    her grace an ever supporting arm
turned out to be the one responsible
    for the greatest amount of harm
his heroic potential was squandered on villainy instead
and a relationship was buried lifeless and dead
the aftermath of the fallout is worse than I can say
what I can be for her is limited but as I go day to day
there is one thing I can do there is one thing I can be
there is one appropriate responsibility
    that falls directly to me
I'm not her man I'm not her healer
    I'm not her teacher nor her dad
but I'm not a stranger either
    so in truth the one thing I'm glad
is that I'm her brother she's my sister and that is worth a lot
we're in the same family and together what we've got
is a holy community of brothers and sisters
    who always defend always lift
that is my role for her that is my God given gift

Good Words Fly

If it's worth saying it's worth saying now
there is no better time and don't worry about how
you think you want to say it just get it said
let those important words fly they're no good in your head
no fear no shame no cowardice no doubt
if it's true then turn it loose if it's good get it out
this may be your only chance
      don't let the opportunity squander
if you happen to be wrong make amends but don't wonder
if you should say it or not
loosen your tongue when it is good
      don't let a thing see you caught

Medicinal Honesty

I hate being honest but there's one thing I hate more
and that would be failing - I hate that to the core!
so in order to minimize my failures to a minimum
I frequently practice honesty so as not to be repeating them
it's not fun it's not cool
      it is not a source of amusement or pleasure
but apart from painful honesty
      I'm condemned beyond all measure
so I gather a few friends real real close
and give my medicine a proper dose
they accept me as I am far or near
and honesty yields courage at the expense of my fear

Teaching on the Mic

Once upon a time our building got too small
every classroom was filled with kids wall to wall
until I even got the boot from my room too
there simply wasn't enough room for everyone to do
what they needed to do so they sent me to a place
called the auxiliary classroom
      where I'd have sufficient space
that's the stage and it's an interesting place to be
because our stage is in the gym
      where every day they have P.E.
now the challenge I have with the girls and boys
is trying to teach dealing with so much noise
and I'm proud to say that even though I'm alone
things just better 'cause I teach on a microphone
now everything is better as I follow my lesson plan
everyone can hear me with a mic in my hand
the basketballs are bouncing but I don't care
because this mic makes my voice fill the air
I don't yell I don't holler I can make the better choice
I let the mic do all work I let the tech raise my voice
and I never knew how much I'd like
the hilarious blessing of teaching on the mic

Fear and Comfort

Sometimes I think of good things to do
      that I haven't done yet
things within expected boundaries
      but also things that could get
me in to trouble with the powers that be
who may or may not see things as I see
but regardless of whether or not men think it's okay
there are two villains in fact
      who tend to keep my good ideas at bay
it is fear and comfort - it is everything they're about
these two frequently keep me from stepping out
fear convinces me the risk is too great
that I'd be better off if I would just wait
the task is too big someone else should get it done
best to stay down I'm not the one
comfort is just as sinister wanting me to stay
in chaos disorder brokenness and disarray
remaining in what I have no reason for remaining
explaining what I have no business explaining
these two are unacceptable and they need to be gone
they construct structures of death and I need to move on

Opportunities Missed Once

If you go to sleep before you do what you meant to do
you can do it when you wake up - it's true
if you're discouraged because you didn't do Plan A
do Plan B or Plan C whatever one you're on today
opportunities missed once are not missed forever
who knows? you may find that the later time
      ends up being better

Lifted Above

Be lifted up above temptations
above unmet expectations
above stress anxiety and worry
above harried days filled with hurry
above the have tos could haves and shoulds
above the envy for others' goods
above failure fear and defeat
above getting bashed bruised and beat
above consequences that none can afford
when we humble ourselves before the Lord

Dusty Inventory

When your shelves get full and threaten to bust
and everything on them collects nothing but dust
it's probably time to evaluate your inventory
and take a shot at steering your story
in a direction better suited for success
and since your stocked shelves are already a mess
just sell it trade it or even give it away
you haven't used it in years so you probably won't today
I bet it will even put a smile on your face
to look at your shelves and see so much space
no hoarding no clutter easier on the eyes a better flow
if there is no vacancy on your shelves
      do yourself a favor and let it go

Treasure You

Many words straddle the fence
        concerning their part of speech
I love pointing this out to my students
        in the classroom as I teach
and there is no shortage of examples
        for me to relay the measure
but the one that has currently captured my attention
        is the noun verb treasure
and the side receiving my current attraction
is the side that expresses the action
treasure can be what you have but it is also what you do
it is what you do with people and memories
        that mean the most to you
there are so many souls of infinite worth
that deserve to be treasured here on earth
I think of my wife my children my mom and dad
my brothers and my friends
        and so many who make me glad
I treasure every last one of them for that's what they are
I hold them in my heart and even when they're far
I treasure them until theory becomes practice
reunited joyfully and the simple fact is
I don't have to be near the ones I love so much
in order for me to treasure them I can do it without a touch
without a word without a thing but my heart
when it comes to treasuring do you know the best part?
the best part is that treasuring someone is done on the whole
I treasure those who share affinities to the soul
and there is no counterfeiting that nor is there a substitute
if I treasure you then know
        we are kindred spirits same heart same root

Adequacy

Adequacy almost always seems just out of reach
the moment I think I've got it
      is the moment that life will teach
me once again that I am inadequate still
despite my resolve determination and will
and I guess I should expect it by now -
      how else could it possibly go?
if I was adequate for every task
      how would I possibly grow?
on some levels I'm thankful for my many inadequacies
for it is these by the truckloads that bring me to my knees
and all the adequacy I can imagine is found in such a place
beaming just beaming upon His perfectly glorious face
in His presence my adequacy doesn't stand a chance
my adequacy limps along while His rises to dance
my adequacy gets knocked down when tasks are too tough
my adequacy is insufficient His is perfectly enough

Discovery

There's something about discovery that moves and propels
the discoverer to anticipation that grows and swells
because every little bit leads to the goal
of all that is partial becoming whole
so that were not just seeing a little here a little there
we're seeing the whole thing - all of it everywhere
what has been discovered now that our work is through?
the whole thing as it is in its form that is true

Take em Along

Sometimes I make excuses as to why I can't pitch in
and help with this or that and the latest one has been
the fact that I'm a dad and I still have a little one
and watching my fella becomes a reason
      I've let some things go undone
it sounds awful to admit and I am for sure not proud
because I'm missing an opportunity
      to put little buddy in a good crowd
my consolation is that I am not always this way
in fact I could have made excuses in regard to yesterday
but I resolved to man up and take my three along
and the four of us found a happier song
by doing what's right three children and their Dad
and between you and me I couldn't be more glad

Love Bombs

The only thing more dangerous than fear is love
fear is strong but love is above
all others in terms of what it can render
fear is a tight wad but love is a spender
fear is a chain but love is a bomb
fear is a stranger but love is a mom
or a dad or a husband or a wife
fear is death but love is life
and life is blowing up like I've never known before
fear won some battles but love won the war
and I was so scared so scared I wouldn't get through
so scared the chains of fear
      would asphyxiate my soul but love knew
love knew what I needed in order to conquer my fear
these love bombs broke the fear chains that bind
      and fear is not welcome here
he knows it oh he knows it very well
and he also knows that when he tries to return
      he can just go to hell
love has no time for fear and all that he assails
love is always stronger than fear fear falters
      but love never fails

Sin Management

Sin management is an art in which many excel
presenting a healthy front
      even when we're anything but well
we all do it - deception is the norm
burning on the inside running PR for our storm
guarded to the greatest extent with contentment on our face
we're not broken we're not hurting
      we don't need help nor grace
how sad is it? how tragic to appear so alive?
how unfortunate it is to mistake this for means to survive
when all we need is one just one set of listening ears
just one shoulder to bury our face
      and cry some much needed tears
oh it's messy it's embarrassing it is no fun to feel so down
but when we mess up and we all mess up
      it's so much better to have someone around
there is life to be found in strength not our own
sin managers can hit the road because this is not done alone

Monotheistic Encouragement

The universe is not polytheistic
    and that is a really good thing
realizing it in its fullness
    is enough make you dance and sing
reality is monotheistic meaning there's only one God
and that is better news than you may have considered
    so good you may applaud
because sometimes the way we speak and think
    is rather polytheistic
in the spiritual realm there are many beings
    and you can be optimistic
that even though we have an enemy
    there is something our enemy is not
our enemy is not a god and that is worth a lot
because we also have a Friend and that Friend is very large
it is God Who is our Friend and He is the One in charge

Vengeance in Me

I have a score to settle with someone who has hurt me a lot
someone who knew better but did it anyway and got caught
up in himself and everything he never needed to be
I'm a bit of an expert because I'm talking about me
and you might say that this is a vengeance story
and it's not about pride vanity or glory
but the fact that my old self has hurt me so much
his words his actions his thoughts his very touch
make me want to stand and say
that vengeance is mine and he's gonna pay
but as soon as I say such things I have another thought
that it is not my hand
      through which vengeance must be brought
it's actually more beautiful what I'm saying is
that vengeance isn't mine vengeance is His
He even says so it's in The Word
and it's downright silly stupid and absurd
to think that I've hurt myself as much as I've hurt Him
He loves me more than I love myself His Light is never dim

God I need You today I need You to deal with my past
I need You to handle my laziness my pride
      these things don't need to last
I need You to handle my deception my isolation
      and my self-centeredness
God I need You to handle all of my rebellion
      all of my sin it's a mess
I need You to settle the score on the things that I used to be
fill me with Your Holy Fire take Your vengeance in me

Reaching for the Pen (for Daniel Tomlinson)

I've been reaching for the pen for more than twenty years
expressing hopes disappointments victories and fears
and every time I meet someone else who shares my art
it is a remarkable blessing to my soul mind and heart
there is only one thing better
        than someone who does the same
and that is the connection to a writer
        when that writer shares my name
I come from writers the full cycle of literacy demonstrated
        by my father and mother
and I can't say enough about the connection I enjoy
        with my oldest brother
we are some writing fools sometimes paper
        sometimes screen
we find great satisfaction through expression
        of abstract thoughts becoming seen
we're fans of each other we follow comment like and share
no shyness in our mutual love
        we're more than proud to declare
I'm more than proud to call this man my bro
and today I find even more reasons than how we flow
today we celebrate the day he was born
and my great satisfaction is publicly worn
I want the world to know what this man means to me
because not only do we reach for the pen there is something
else that has come to be
we reach for each other we have each other's backs
he's seen some dark days for me and he didn't relax
he held me up so today I do the same
here's to my big brother Daniel so proud we share one name

Blessed Conflict

Conflict is a blessing - yeah you heard me right
when two forces are in opposition
      and they both exert their might
in order to determine which one emerges victorious
everybody wants to hear about the winner
      and what his story is
and without the conflict there's no winner
      without the winner there's no story to hear
and if there's no winner's story
      how are we gonna get better this year
that's why having a winner leaves no second guessing
that is why I believe conflict is a blessing

They Stay

I'm so thankful for friends and family
      that hold my feet to the fire
tell me what I never want to hear and never ever retire
when I get stupid and completely self centered
walking down paths that should never be entered
they don't leave me even though I deserve it
they don't make fun of me even though they could serve it
up on a regular basis it's true
it's safe to say they've tasted grace
      and they've got eternity in view
it's safe to say they're the safest folks I have ever met
God sent for sure these people are my safety net
and God knows my history reveals
      a tendency to fall off the line
but these people these beautiful people
      are there to catch me every time
which brings me to a place of gratitude
      thanksgiving and appreciation
the plants that yield the fruits of healing
      and reset my life's animation
toward the One who brought us together in the first place
the One Who never leaves the One Who shows grace

What You Do

Do what you do
don't do what they do
they do what they do
so we don't need you to do it too
no one can do that thing that you do
and if you don't do it it'll never get done

Friend of a Friend

A friend of a friend is still a friend
they may be less known but that's not how it has to end
I've been rewarded by investments made
with returns that didn't spoil or fade
when one degree of separation was eliminated
and a new friendship was created
by the common fellowship we were already holding
layers of friendship began unfolding
to reveal a richness present but as yet unobserved
it makes sense really once it all gets served
with domestic and spiritual blessings to boot
kindness and character are the fruit
of my friend who is such a blessing to know
this friend of a friend my friend is good to go

Drink some Water

Step on dirt
drink water
that's how it's supposed to go
but things get twisted in reverse sometimes
things go fast that wanna go slow
things go left when they wanna go right
you get darkness when you ordered light
the only thing to do when craziness sets in
is to get back up out of the dirt and drink some water again

Tune In

Tune out on what doesn't matter to tune in on what does
it may be a temptation to tune it all out
      but that would be bad because
there are still some things worth tuning in to
well not things exactly but it's those in view
it's people it's the people you're next to every day
it's your family and friends that have the power to stay
your attention when it wants to roam free
and play among the distractions that ensnare so easily
tuning in will anchor you like a tether
distractions pass on by as we tune in together

Better Living

It's a little bit of him and a little bit of me
all the way us I'm so thankful to see
we're doing being hanging and going
11 almost 12 he shows no signs of slowing
down so we take every chance we get
and every chance we make is towards it
getting better all the time which is very short
but as of these events I'm happy to report
that we didn't waste the hours we were given
they were invested in better livin'
much more than my words this is what will remain
what we did together will stick in his brain
his heart his mind his soul
and to that end we press to goal

The Necessity of Words

If it's the same then words are useless
but if it's different then words are excessive
discernment is found in the tension
between words that could and words that must
the necessity of words is much more subtle
     than anyone can imagine
only One can lay claim to having discerned
     every spoken opportunity correctly
and He was more known for what He did than what He said

Uncover the Glory

It's no secret that I'm a fan of fire in the fall
but our fire pit gets overgrown when it's not used at all
and ends up a lawn mowing obstacle in our backyard
far from its original purpose its usefulness is marred
a look out the kitchen window just makes me sad
because grassy fireless fire pits are just plain bad
it takes the right combination of people and planning
to uncover the glory of campfire flames fanning
what a sight in the October night sky
friends good food I sit back and sigh
taking it all in what a way for a day to end
before the grass sprouts in my fire pit
      let's be sure and do this again

Pro-Choice Pro-Life

Two kinds of good guys locked in each others' crosshairs
both right in their own minds consumed by exclusive cares
to the degree that the only sound they hear
      is their own voice
far from the ideals they preach
      are those who are pro-life and pro-choice
a political distinction lacking relevance as much as merit
significantly self-righteous and I will no longer bear it
because neither one is worthy
      of the labels they rally behind
they suppose their morality is vindicated
      by their correct political mind
but what is right can only be understood by what we do
and we cannot claim pro choice or pro life
      if these are not the things we pursue
we can call ourselves pro choice when
we acknowledge the rights of unborn women and men
when we publicize choices to the desperate in our nation
that do not cause a life's termination
when we abandon the facade that spoils and blights
the lie dressed up as women's rights
when we stop caring in theory and practice it instead
only then will we be pro-choice in truth
      and not just in our head
and the right wingers for sure are just as bad
we have failed the unborn and it is sadder than sad
where's the rage? where's the anger?
      where's the righteous indignation?
if we are pro-life for the unborn in our nation
we will be pro-life when we divorce the shame
from pregnancy to how the conception came
when we blur the lines between the races and the classes
and look at all men through God tinted glasses

when we take our fight from debating the facts
to loving those on the other side of the tracks
when we stop conditioning our sons and daughters to be
terrified of getting caught
that the only thing they can think of doing
    is resorting to a murder bought

Our hypocrisy is evident God have mercy please
may we lay down our empty ideals
    to love the least of these

Leaving Home

Kryptonians don't have powers on Krypton
there's something about leaving home
    that turns their power on
evidently the Earth's sun activates heat vision
    strength and flight
making them amazing super even able to win every fight
that's the story of Kal-El better known as Superman
the preeminent superhero on the planet
    if no one is able he can
because all he has to do every day
is save everyone and make sure they're okay
because he's not going home he's not gonna run
he's gonna be here until the job gets done
and even then he's gonna be around
in the sky and all over the ground
he can focus on others high and low
he ain't worried about going home
    because he left home a long time ago

Shoes

House shoes are great if you're not going anywhere
and I guess if you have a quick morning errand
    they're okay to wear
but I wouldn't suggest wearing them all day
they're not gonna support you as you make your way
through work competition escape and pursuits
house shoes won't do you need running shoes or work boots
house shoes won't help you win the race
racing in house shoes will destroy your pace
house shoes won't protect you at construction sites
they're sure to lose all accidental fights
work boots are winners sure to succeed
giving your feet the armor they're sure to need
if you're going somewhere
    leave your house shoes by your bed
and let your feet be ready for what lies ahead

All Go to War

Six warlords hovering over the face of the earth
the acquisition of continents defining their worth
to the point that the only purpose
     is for all others to be dominated
victory won when all others are eliminated
I was a fool to imagine victory within reach
serving as a negative example to teach
everyone else not to lift up their head
before the conqueror we all were dead
the map filled with one color from east to west
six became one because one was the best
the vanity of the risk was clear for us five
all go to war but only one will survive

Held in the Arms

The disappointments of man are more than I can count
our transgressions mistakes and failures are an ever
increasing amount
my feelings of safety waver from day to day
and between friends family and acquaintances I know of
none to whom I can say
what it is that burdens me so deep
pain that invades my lightest consciousness
      to my deepest sleep
there is only One I can trust and the only thing left to do
is to run into everlasting arms and hide myself in You
You Who knit me together in my mother's womb
possess proprietary understanding when alone in my room
and my loneliness comes to stay in order to remind
that You are enough and You are close enough to find
save whatever may be at hand or in my head
Your Spirit wraps my fragile heart
      with every single word You've said
I am held in the arms of the One Who gets me
letting my weary heavy laden heart rest
      I am exactly where I need to be

Rooted in God's Desire

My identity is a blessing rooted in God's desire
His ownership is the spark that lights a blazing fire
that has been burning from before the world's foundation
with holiness and purity my destiny is my destination
confidence? position? election? all of the above!
I am branded with the sign of ownership Divine Love
is the only way I have such freedom such emancipation
He adopted me because He wanted to
      it is His work that is my salvation
He wants me and His election is a pleasure
that's a treasure for which there is no measure
there is no way to capture a proper understanding
of His magnanimity His grace His truth commanding
He has the control not me and He never will retire
and my identity need never be shaken
      for it is rooted in God's desire

Back to the Basics

When distractions become so attractive
that my impulses become so hyperactive
it's time to wind it back a decade or two
and remember what first made me true
because the basics haven't been rearranged
basically the basics are still the same
it's that the departure I took clouded my view
and my perspective on the basics couldn't get through
until I removed what was in the way
to discover they'd been here every day
what a sweet observation to be able to taste this
feels so good to get back to the basics

No Way

There's no such thing as too many tickle fights
too much frisbee tossing or too many wind kites
you can never enough kisses or hugs
or wrestling matches on living room rugs
or rock me to sleeps or carry me to bed
or big belly laughs over funny things said
too much no matter what his mood
there is no way to have too much of this dude

These Words

These words are the representatives sent by my emotions
writing laws and carrying motions
that give my ideas a form and a voice
a path to discover a beautiful choice
to bless the fluidity from my mind to my heart
such a description is fitting for the art
that provides the structure for my expression
and as long as this continues to be my impression
I will keep on and I don't expect that to change
so I will write recite edit and arrange
these words that reveal wherever I may be
I'd do it come what may but thanks for listening to me

Always Be Here

If you don't make it it won't exist
and if it doesn't exist how will it persist
when times grow thin from wear and tear
and the rawness of it not being there
if you make it make it your own
better yet don't make it alone
make it with your family or friend
make it together and the time you spend
won't actually be spent but rather invested
if you know what I'm thinking of you may have guessed it
and yes it is a thing but it also represents
huge significance in this present tense
that cannot go away or even disappear
if you make it it will always be here

Mountains Speak to Valleys

Mountains speak to valleys what is to what is not
what rises above to what falls below the movement to the
trapped in thought
sometimes it hurts when my highs have to speak to my lows
but if that conversation never takes place
      then you know how it goes
straight down to the bottom with no hope for getting out
flat on my back eyes filled with gray skies
      forever lost in doubt
I will engineer my victories to tweak my frequent defeats
and level the playing field one day at a time
      to travel down enlightened streets

Exceeding Greatness

God's power is toward us who believe
and its measure for us to receive
is not based on me or you
but according to the working of His mighty power it's true
the power He used to raise His Son
and seat Him at His right hand it was done
and Jesus on the throne is above everything
this move succeeded and what did it bring?
it brought every principality power and might
under Him Who authored the Light
and every name named right now and right here
is subject to Him this month and this year
and the year after that and the year after that
what I'm saying what I'm getting at
is that God in Christ wrote the book on working hard
no further work needed no need to post a guard
it has already been taken care of it is already done
the exceeding greatness of His power toward us simply
means that we have already won

Prepared Beforehand

It's late Monday night and He's already out there
thinking planning orchestrating
    and developing with great care
the opportunities that He wants me to walk in
the chances to demonstrate His great love
    to all the women and men
that He created in His image we are image bearers
and because of this and because of Him
    we can be workers and sharers
with anyone and everyone that has too little or not enough
not enough hope not enough love not enough food
    or not enough stuff
that's an opportunity for us to be hands and feet
God touched moments where the rubber
    touches down on my street
open doors to minds and hearts all lead by His command
all hearts leaning in to life
    because of what He prepared beforehand

Everything I Need (Scarecrow's Defense)

Liars cheaters and thieves
      want to take what is rightfully mine
but in order for them to successfully cross the line
there is one thing which they must convince
and that is of the inadequacy of my defense
regardless of whether or not what they say is true
their purpose is to take what's mine
      by warping my clear view
I want to remember that their words are lies indeed
my defense is not inadequate
      and I already have everything I need

The Dry Gray Place

The dry gray place is home but is that where you belong?
in this land over the rainbow you've learned a different song
influenced by the wonderful colors
     of the wondrous landscape sights
the beauty of it all is perfectly evident a 1001 delights
and yet the familiarity of home continually beckons
old dry gray home is offering you seconds
but is home best is home really it
is home really what you want or are you trying to get
something that you already possess
you may want to pause for a second guess
there's no place like home that's true to the letter
but a place not like home in the end could be better

Adorable Trick-or-Treater

Give a bag and costume to a two year old
and watch a night that's solid gold
little buddy's first trick-or-treating
      was all the sugar I needed
such an adorable experience I can promise you
      it will be repeated
because he figured out what he had to do
      to get a ton of candy
it was dark outside and he was tired
      but everything was fine and dandy
his cuteness sparked wonder and he became our little leader
once again so thankful for our adorable trick-or-treater

Wonders Never Cease

It is a gift to be included in the work of God's creation
God the Creator the Artist
    the One Who invented inspiration
is using us as a medium for Divine self expression
and despite us it is my impression
that He is achieving success
    through the work of His hands and mind
I am absolutely astounded and the words that I want to find
are out there beyond me in a place I cannot reach
because His creativity stretching from mountain to beach
chose to use us in fact we are His masterpiece
mankind humanity His wonders never cease

A Gift to Pass On

What is all this for if not to bless?
the technology the creativity is much more than less
an avenue through which the masses can be inspired
empowered for greatness and ultimately hired
by the passion from within the drive from their core
that defining action that they were created for
I feel it when my expression breaks through someone's day
that otherwise was headed down a bad way
but a word or a motion helped them hold on
to something deep inside that was never really gone
I feel it when when I see the lights come on in their mind
when clarity clears ambiguity and sight comes to the blind
when I do anything that gets the spotlight off of me
onto others who are much more brave and courageous than
I could ever be
all of this that we're given from the best to the worst
is a gift to pass on and put others first

He is Our Peace

Even if we agree that doesn't mean we get along
we could share the same belief
      and still treat each other wrong
and really there's not a person I know
that I agree with all the time so
I say all that to say that peace is not something I can make
and if it is it really isn't if you think it is it's really fake
peace is not man made rather peace is given
and here on this planet among the land of the livin
there is only One who can give peace true
only One engineer that harmonizes me and you
and the only reason this is the case
is because Peace is a person with a name and a face
there is so much hope for me and you
because Peace is not what Peace is Who
and between you and I the love doesn't ever have to cease
He has made it so for He Himself is our peace

United Nations

Differences pushed aside for the sake of what we're
pursuing
peace and human dignity ever practicing ever doing
we remember what it was like when we were not united
and the levels of fear and panic rose
    when we were all divided
and not to say that these seventy years
    have been anything close to perfection
but it can be said that our union
    is a step in the right direction
people groups looking after one another
acknowledging that despite our differences
    you're my sister and my brother
and if you're in trouble I'm gonna do everything I can
to get you out of your crisis - we'll make a plan
and come together without hesitations
demonstrating our own name
    showing the world United Nations

Won and Winning

Traditionally many of us consider it a beginning
but the truth of it is that on the day
      we are actually a long time winning
because it is our point in time intersecting with infinity
a mysterious inheritance marked by one third of The Trinity
there is no way to classify something
      that affects the future present and past
I'm talking about the choice that was made
      that secured a destiny fast
a decision to yield an entire reality
      an entire frame of perception
to the Master the Author the Maker
      the Deliverer of the second conception
the beauty of the moment isn't confined to one day
the blood that flows knows no limits
      it is not restricted to just one way
but in around over and through it covers fills and erases
the Son of God is He Who saves with Mercy
      and infinite Graces
a victory won a life begun
      and wonderful tale in the spinning
death to life risen forever overwhelmed
      among the ageless perpetually winning

Person VS Technology

I like people - I really do
but sometimes the way I behave
    makes it seem like that's not true
sometimes it probably seems like
    the primary focus focus for me
is the little device I use so much my portable technology
the disengagement the distraction
    the allure of its pixels and sound
it's always near always available always present
    when I want it around
admittedly it is dangerous for its appeal is ever near
it is difficult for me to be the one
    who does the right thing here
person versus technology - oh that's a tough one
but with help from friends and family
    the conflicting matter is surely won

Hope for Compassion

It's that sense of suffering alongside
that quality of brother-keeping though not in the tide
but not letting that matter the least little bit
and still choosing to intentionally be a part of all of it
suffering with I admit
    it's not something we automatically choose
but when we need it it's always something
    we hope for others to use
compassion - easily defined easily received received
    but never easy to give
few have tasted it to its fullness among those who still live
because hopefully compassion is a boomerang
    blessing those who share it
hopefully compassion goes viral and defines all who wear it
but if it does not and if compassion is a snare unto death
then those who die with the gospel of compassion
    uttered in their last breath
will have lived fuller lives than all others who refrained
swallowed up in Life Victory attained

Big Brother Little Brother

Early on it was just him he was our one little dude
delightful in nearly every way and mostly in a good mood
soon enough he was the oldest with two precious others
I can't imagine anyone better
      to hold the title of best big brother
At some point he crossed over
      from the natural to the spiritual
and I went from being over him to being his equal
my son became my brother
      when he surrendered his will eternally
sharing one Father united in the Spirit
      bound in uniform destiny
these two states of brotherhood sum up who he is
      and who will be
big brother little brother who means the world to me

Exhale Gratitude

I'm not done being thankful I hope to never be
I hope to never put limits on the gratitude
    that is the breath and life of me
breathe gratitude - man - I like the sound of that
there's wisdom in expressing my thanks
    no matter where I'm at
inhale blessing exhale gratitude
entitlement selfishness and vain conceit
    are burned by such an attitude
my hard heart is softened when tempted by such attractions
they only exist in gratitude's absence they're not the thing
they're just the attraction
and with the healing flood of gratitude
    they are washed away
yielding contentment but not content
    to remain in just one day

Peace Deep Inside

The noise seems the loudest when there's no noise at all
just leftovers in my head echoes of every call
from everyone and everything clamoring for my attention
some large some small but they all lead to the suspension
of peace that wants to flow through every inch of my being
but there are so many roadblocks and dams it is just
obstacles that I'm seeing
I honestly don't know how to change this or make it alright
I suspect silence cannot be won in a moment's pursuit
she is only captured by hearts at the root
casual chasers are always denied
peace is granted to those willing to seek her deep inside

Blast the Spotlight

My default is candid introspection
an emotional pulse check to observe the direction
of my thoughts and feelings my head and heart
therapeutic aesthetics - not a bad start
that's where it's been I speak as one that knows
but I also have seen where it goes
and it goes out much more than than it comes in
the next level is realized and it is such a win
that I am compelled to do it evermore
and not just examine and reexamine my core
not just give an emotional report
but use this to create encouragement and support
to sharpen heighten and blast the spotlight
on everyone doing everything right

Thanks

Leah, Landon, Hannah, Nathan, Mom, Dad, Daniel, Joel, Jeremy, Papa, Meme, Adam, Mary Jo, Stephen and Joanna Dixon, Kevin and Kara Capps, Brandon and Cindy Riggan, Damon and Leigh Anne Hancock, Rob Carris, Brian Brophy, Carl Johnson, Brett Emerson, Chris Waterman, Community Church of Hendersonville, Arthur Alligood, Wayne and Stacy Brezinka, Doug and Diane Zimmerman, Joe and Nelia Waldrum, Amy Tenney, Mark and Jackie Branstetter, Kody and Jessica Woodard, Doug and Linda Varnado, Chris and Cindy Long, Justin and Lacy McKay, Gidget Stewart, Fresh Start, Steve Brown, Hendersonville Samaritan Association, George Pendergrass, Heather Lawson, Kevin Lawson, Cedarstone School of Music, Justin Swanson, Hendersonville Martial Arts, Ricky and Micol Davis, Jimmy Travis, Tia Mitchell, Rashad Rayford, Minton Sparks, Crystal Jones, Raichon Morand, Courtney Nichols, Jessica Shrum, Jerry Skaggs, Kurt, Jeanine, Dane and Ava McBee, Tom and Sandy Koentop, David and Michelle Nimmo, Darren and Kim Frank, Darrell and Kendra Lassiter, Clark Flatt, The Jason Foundation, Chuck Swann, Monica and Dean Darbyshire, Tennessee Pour House, Uncommon Grounds, Portland Brew East, Ben Smith, Southern Word, Lee and Melody Bowling, Renae and L.T. Hudson, Waylon Carey, Nolan and Alisha Crooks, Stone Bresnahan, Chris Seward, Noah Collier, Riley Mills, Antonio Garner, Nick Darbyshire, Ryan Voss, Jenny Stiles, Amy Joley, Susan Odom, Becky Auen, Blake and Sarah Southall, Candy Mitchell, Brittany Johnson, Station Camp Middle School, Westmoreland Middle School, Sumner County Schools, Kayren Craighead, Emily Mofield, Ales Dvorak, Pam Holdcraft, Pam Davenport, Alison Robinson, Paula Kiggins, Susan Clendenen, and you.

Thank you for your encouragement, participation, support and love.